PRESCHOOL TEACHER'S
MONTH-by-MONTH
Activities
Program

Lorraine
Clancy

**THE CENTER FOR APPLIED
RESEARCH IN EDUCATION**
West Nyack, New York 10995

Library of Congress Cataloging-in-Publication Data

Clancy, Lorraine.
    Preschool teacher's month-by-month activities program / Lorraine
Clancy.
       p.   cm.
   ISBN 0–87628–632–5
    1. Education, Preschool—United States—Activity programs—
Handbooks, manuals, etc.   2. Preschool teaching—Handbooks,
manuals, etc.   3. Teaching—Aids and devices—Handbooks, manuals
etc.   I. Title.
LB1140.35.C74C55   1991
372.11'02—dc20   90–23326
                                               CIP

ISBN 0-87628-632-5

THE CENTER FOR APPLIED
RESEARCH IN EDUCATION
BUSINESS & PROFESSIONAL DIVISION
A division of Simon & Schuster
West Nyack, New York 10995

Printed in the United States of America

About the Author

Lorraine Clancy received her B.S. in preschool and Early Childhood Education from the State University at Old Westbury, New York. She is presently teaching preschool at St. Joseph's School in Garden City, New York, a program she began in 1980.

Mrs. Clancy has taught creative crafts workshops for early childhood teachers, as well as summer classes for children. She has written a curriculum workshop article for *Today's Catholic Teacher* entitled "Art in Early Childhood Education." She is also the author of *Seasonal Arts and Crafts for Early Childhood* (Parker Publishing Company, 1988) and is a contributor to *The Primary Teacher's Ready-to-Use Activities Program* (a monthly publication published by The Center for Applied Research in Education.)

About This Resource

The Preschool Teacher's Month-by-Month Activities Program places in your hands hundreds of stimulating classroom activities and over 150 reproducible activity pages and patterns to help you plan an effective and exciting preschool program from September through May/June.

For your convenience, all of this ready-to-use teaching material is organized into nine monthly sections and is printed in a big 8½" x 11" spiral-bound format that folds flat for easy photocopying. The student activity pages and patterns can be reproduced just as they are, as many times as needed, for use with individual children, small groups of students with similar needs or interests, or your entire class.

You'll find you can use this unique resource as the basis for developing an effective preschool program of your own, or as a means to enhance and reinforce an existing program. It begins with "An Organized Day," a suggested format on which you can build your daily schedule. The essential aspects of the "Organized Day" include step-by-step suggestions for setting up and running your own program. The "Approximate Time" table in an "Organized Day" helps you manage your time and organize your activities. A tested and effective floor plan, along with a list of preschool materials, equipment, and furnishings will be help in setting up a new preschool classroom. Suggested materials for interest centers will add a creative and efficient aspect to your room. Cooking in the classroom is explored and simple recipes are included. Name tags, birthday crowns and monthly "Beginnings" (newsletter to parents) help your program run smoothly from start to finish.

The "Helpers Chart" shows you how to set up a motivating bulletin board that can build skills and teach responsibility. The easy "Name Train" begins your children on the road to letter and name recognition while giving your children that warm feeling that *this* is MY room.

The program contains over 250 exciting, ready-to-use classroom and individual activities to add creative, skill-building fun to your preschool curriculum from the opening of school in September till it closes in May or June. Each chapter concludes with suggestions for Music/Movement Activities, finger plays, games, songs and poems.

Each monthly section also includes a number of music and movement activities appropriate to the month as well as special holiday and seasonal projects that are sure to bring extra excitement to your classroom.

Preschool children possess a natural curiosity about life. Following the stimulating month-by-month activities in this resource your children will be looking, listening, touching, creating, moving, singing, and experiencing life. Inherent in the curriculum is the development of your students' essential childhood skills and attitudes toward their environment and toward themselves.

Lorraine Clancy

Contents

About This Resource iii

THE ORGANIZED DAY 1

A Time Frame for Activities 2

Name Tags 2

Room Arrangement and Materials 3

Cooking in the Classroom 8

Helpers' Chart 9

The Counter 10

Name Train 10

Calendar 13

Snack Time 14

Sharing 15

Storytime   **15**

Letters to Parents   **16**

Birthday Crown   **16**

WELCOME TO SEPTEMBER!   **19**

Beginnings   **20**

September Storytime   **21**

Readiness Activities for September   **22**

> Me in Preschool (22) • Mosaic Apple (22) • Pussy Willows (22) • Clay or Salt Dough Gingerbread Boy or Girl (23) • A Paper Gingerbread Boy or Girl (23) • The Gingerbread Boy's Raisins (23) • Community Helper—Animal Shelter Worker (23) • A Paper Cat or Dog (24) • Cute-as-a-Button Needs Ears (24) • Seeds, Seeds (24) • Observe Growth (24) • Plants Need Light (26) • Plants Need Water (26) • We All Need Water (26) • A September Tree (27) • A Is for Apple (27) • My Number Book (27) • About Me (27) • A "Me" Poster (27) • Button's Number Blocks (27) • What's Missing? (28)

Shape Recognition   **28**

> Fall Rectangle Frame (29) • Shape Chain (30) • Shape Collage (31) • "Shapey" (31) • Silly Shapes (32)

Music and Movement   **36**

> The Hokeypokey (36) • Did You Ever See a Lassie? (36) • Preschool Fitness Album (36)

Contents

Songs, Poems, and Fingerplays   36

Where Is Thumbkin? (36) • Ten Fingers (37) • My Turtle (37) • Little Bird
(37)

From Button's Country Kitchen   38

Gingerbread Cookies (38) • Applesauce (38)

Videos for September   38

Three Richard Scarry Animal Nursery Tales (38) • Little Toad to the Rescue
(38)

Worksheets for September   38

OCTOBER—THE BEWITCHING MONTH   53

Beginnings   54

October Storytime   55

Readiness Activities for October   57

Let's Build a Haunted House (57) • Follow-the-Numbers Pumpkin (57) • G
Is for Ghost (57) • How Many Jack-o'-Lanterns on the Fence? (58) • Carrots
(58) • Pumpkin and Jack-o-Lantern Mask (58) • Build a Witch (59) • Smiley
and Sad (59) • Spiders, Spiders (59) • Grow Carrot Greenery (59) • Grow a
Pineapple Plant (60) • An Acorn Person (60) • Chlorophyll (60) • A Leaf's
Veins (61) • Squirrel Watch (62) • Nuts and More Nuts! (62) • Football
Mums (62) • Sizes of Pumpkins (62) • The Eensy, Weensy Spider (63) •
Popcorn (63) • Nut Hunt (63) • Cat and Mouse Game (63)

Letter Recognition   **64**

Sandpaper A (*64*) • Craft Stick A (*64*) • Rectangle A (*65*) • The As Are Hiding (*65*)

Music and Movement   **65**

I'm a Little Acorn (*65*) • The Tightrope Walker (*65*) • All Fall Down (*65*) • Acorn Roll (*65*)

Songs, Poems, and Fingerplays   **66**

One, Two, Buckle My Shoe (*66*) • Fall (*66*) • Two Little Blackbirds (*66*)

From Button's Country Kitchen   **66**

Orange Brew (*66*) • Orange Gelatin (*67*) • Brownies (*67*) • Toasted Pumpkin Seeds (*67*)

Videos for October   **67**

The Ugly Duckling (*67*)

Worksheets for October   **67**

NOVEMBER—A HARVEST OF FUN   **85**

Beginnings   **86**

November Storytime   **87**

Readiness Activities for November   **88**

Tilly Turtle (*88*) • Feeling "Raisiny" (*88*) • Wattles the Turkey (*88*) • Community Helper—The Police Officer (*84*) • My School and Me (*84*) • "Sour Grapes" (*89*) • An Apple Puzzle (*90*) • Fishing for Your Dinner (*90*) • Indian Corn (*90*) • Vegetables—Above and Below (*90*) • All the Colors of the Rainbow (*91*) • Fun With Peanuts (*91*) • Yummy Peanuts (*92*) • The Peanut Scientist (*92*) • Rainbow Trout Fish Kite (*92*) • My Thanksgiving Book (*92*) • Friends (*92*) • Breakfast, Lunch, and Dinner (*93*) • Fill the Cornucopia (*93*)

Music and Movement   93

Autumn's Here (*93*) • Row, Row, Row Your Canoe (*94*)

Songs, Poems, and Fingerplays   94

Turkey's Song (*94*) • Way Up in an Apple Tree (*94*) • Ten Little Indians (*94*) • Turkeys One and All (*94*)

From Button's Country Kitchen   95

Baking Powder Biscuits (*95*) • Apple Crisp (*95*) • Cinnamon Toast (*95*) • Baked Apples (*95*) • Corn Bread (*96*)

Videos for November   96

The Little Red Hen (*96*)

Worksheets for November   96

ENCHANTING DECEMBER   115

Beginnings   116

December Storytime   117

Readiness Activities for December   118

The Triangle Tree (*118*) • P.J. the Christmas Bear (*118*) • A Dreidel Chain (*118*) • Rudolph Mobile (*119*) • Shhh! (*119*) • Hibernating Worms (*119*) • Hibernating Fish (*119*) • Reddy the Robin (*119*) • Guess Who Belongs to This Foot! (*120*) • Footprint Number Practice (*120*) • Pine Cone Feeder (*120*) • Freckles the Fish (*121*) • A Freckles Mobile (*121*) • Caught Napping (*122*) • Poinsettia (*122*) • Carrot Nose (*122*) • Help Santa Fill the Stocking (*122*) • Santa's Moose (*122*) • D Is for Drum (*122*) • Santa Bag Puppet (*123*) • Rocky the Rocking Horse (*123*) • A December Color Book (*123*) • Santa's Bag (*123*) • Here Comes Winter (*123*) • Holiday Gift Wrap (*123*) • Jingle Bells (*124*) • I Care and Share Medallion (*128*)

Music and Movement   124

Five Little Reindeer Jumping on the Bed (*124*) • Two Little Feet (*125*) • A Listening Game (*125*)

Songs, Poems, and Fingerplays   125

A Fish Ditty (*125*) • Hands on Shoulders (*125*) • Jack in the Box (*126*) • Little Red Caboose (*126*)

From Button's Country Kitchen   126

Matzoh Balls (*126*) • Penny Punch (*126*) • Glue Cookies (*126*)

Videos for December   127

Rudolph the Red-Nosed Reindeer (*127*) • Frosty the Snowman (*127*) • The Little Drummer Boy (*127*)

Worksheets for December   127

JANUARY—A GOOD MONTH FOR DINOSAURS!   **149**

Beginnings   **150**

January Storytime   **151**

Readiness Activities for January   **152**

Stone Footprints (*152*) • Which Dinosaur Is It? (*152*) • How Big Is a "Thunder Lizard"? (*152*) • Dinosaur Eggs (*153*) • The "Flying Dragon" (*153*) • Triceratops (*153*) • Brontosaurus (*154*) • Tyrannosaurus Rex ((*154*) • Stegosaurus Puzzle (*154*) • Going for a Swim (*154*) • Which Is Longer? (*154*) • Which Is Taller? (*155*) • Additional Dinosaur Activities (*155*) • Number Soup (*156*) • P Is for Panda (*156*) • The ABC Cats (*156*) • Ice Cream for You and a Friend (*157*) • Who's Missing? (*157*) • Dr. Martin Luther King, Jr. (*157*) • Snowflakes (*157*) • Snowballs (*158*) • Build an Ice House (*158*) • January Mittens (*158*) • Make a Snowman (*158*) • Mitten Match (*158*)

Music and Movement   **158**

Miss Snowflake (*158*) • If You're Happy and You Know It (*159*) • The Scale Song (*159*) • Playing Prehistorics (*159*)

Songs, Poems, and Fingerplays   **160**

Dinosaurs, We Love You (*160*)

From Button's Country Kitchen   **161**

Bread Pudding (*161*) • Peanut Butter Bread (*161*)

Videos for January   **161**

Mister Rogers Home Video: Dinosaurs and Monsters (*161*) • Digging Up Dinosaurs (*162*) • Dinosaurs, Dinosaurs, Dinosaurs (*162*)

Worksheets for January   **162**

FEBRUARY—LOVE TO ALL   **183**

Beginnings   **184**

February Storytime   **185**

Readiness Activities for February   **186**

Love is Sharing (*186*) • Have a Heart (*186*) • A Rosey Rose (*186*) • My Heart's Aflutter (*186*) • I Give You My Heart (*186*) • Three Hearts (*186*) • Heart Doily (*187*) • Miss (or Mr.) Heart (*187*) • Sponge-Painted Heart (*188*) • Heart Flower (*188*) • Sew a Heart (*189*) • George's Cherry Trees (*189*) • The Height of Abraham Lincoln (*190*) • A Lincoln Medal (*190*) • Let's Make Es (*190*) • E Wants to Eat (*190*) • Woody (*191*) • Woody's Shadow (*191*) • Rectangle Bridges (*191*) • Over and Under the Bridge (*191*) • Shadow Tag (*192*) • What's Missing? (*192*)

Music and Movement   **192**

We Care (*192*) • Shadows (*193*) • Light and Shadows (*193*)

Songs, Poems, and Fingerplays   **193**

Woody's Ditty (*193*)

From Button's Country Kitchen   **193**

George's Miniature Cheese Cakes (*193*) • Marzipan Candy Hearts (*194*)

Videos for February   **194**

The Mother Goose Treasury (*194*) • Polly's Pet (*194*)

Worksheets for February   **194**

MARCH IS BREEZING BY   **205**

Beginnings   **206**

March Storytime   **207**

Readiness Activities for March   **208**

What Is Green? (*208*) • Green Grapes (*208*) • G Is for Grape (*209*) • Green
Snakes (*209*) • Community Helper—Dentist (*209*) • Shaughnessy Shawn's
Hat (*209*) • Grow Shamrocks (*210*) • Green Carnation Greetings (*210*) •
Sponge-Painted Shamrock (*210*) • Shamrock Hunt (*210*) • The Versatile
Potato (*210*) • Mr. or Mrs. Potato (*213*) • Shaughnessy Shawn Bag Puppet
(*213*) • Shaughnessy's Shillelagh (*213*) • Pots of Gold (*213*) • Fun with Air
and Wind (*213*) • Making a Windsock (*214*) • Mary's Lamb (*215*) • The March
Wind (*215*) • A March Kite (*215*)

Music and Movement   **216**

Shaughnessy's Song (*216*) • Shaughnessy's Game (*216*) • The March Wind
(*216*)

Songs, Poems, and Fingerplays   **216**

Mary Had a Little Lamb (*216*) • Baa-Baa Black Sheep (*217*) • Harrigan
(*217*)

From Button's Country Kitchen   **217**

Green Finger Gelatin (*217*) • Johnnycake (*218*)

Videos for March   **218**

5 Lionni Classics (*218*)

Worksheets for March   **218**

APRIL—A SHOWER OF FUN   **235**

Beginnings   **236**

April Storytime   **237**

Readiness Activities for April   **238**

Passover Foods (*238*) • Eggs, Eggs, How Many Eggs? (*238*) • Count and Color (*240*) • Wet Chalk Eggs (*240*) • Cute-as-a-Button Bunny (*241*) • Spring Showers (*241*) • Signs of Spring (*241*) • Raindrops (*241*) • Community Helper—Letter Carrier (*242*) • Be a Philatelist (*242*) • ZIP Codes (*242*) • Observing Spring (*243*) • Miss Caterpillar and Her Cocoon (*243*) • Arbor Day (*243*) • Nature at Work (*243*)

Music and Movement   **244**

A Richard Scarry Record (*244*) • This Old Man (*244*) • Hoppity, Hop (*245*)

Songs, Poems, and Fingerplays   **245**

Open, Shut Them (*245*) • I'm a Little Teapot (*246*)

From Button's Country Kitchen   **246**

> Refrigerator Pudding (*246*) • Carrot Salad (*246*) • Potato Latkes (*246*) • Baked Rice Pudding (*247*)

Videos for April   **247**

> The Velveteen Rabbit (*247*) • The Tale of Peter Rabbit (*247*)

Worksheets for April   **247**

MAY/JUNE—AN UPBEAT ENDING   **255**

Beginnings   **256**

May/June Storytime   **257**

Readiness Activities for May/June   **258**

> Pretty Priscilla the Butterfly (*258*) • F Is for Fish (*259*) • Geraniums (*259*) • A Preschool-Is-Fun Flower (*259*) • Sponge-Painted Lilacs (*259*) • Pretty Petals (*259*) • Ladybug, Ladybug (*260*) • How Old Are You, Ladybug? (*260*) • Community Helper—Utility Employee (*260*) • My Preschool Friends (*261*) • A Sandcastle (*261*) • M Is for Mouse (*261*) • Mother's Day Plaque (*261*) • Father's Day Card (*262*) • Buzzy Bee (*262*) • Fireflies (*262*) • Pasta Chain (*262*) • You and Me, a Math Game (*262*)

Music and Movement   **264**

> Old MacDonald Had a Farm (*264*) • Jack in the Box (*264*) • The Snail (*264*) • Bluebird, Bluebird (*264*)

Songs, Poems, and Fingerplays   **265**

The Wheels on the Bus (*265*) • Little Bird (*265*) • The Little Turtle (*266*)

From Button's Country Kitchen   266

Banana Slush (*266*)

Videos for May/June   266

Good Morning, Good Night: A Day on the Farm (*266*) • The Pokey Little Puppy and the Patchwork Blanket (*266*) • A Day at Old MacDonald's Farm (*267*)

Worksheets for May/June   267

A TIME FRAME FOR ACTIVITIES

Get off to a good start by setting a time frame so that you can accomplish your goals and objectives, while enjoying the children and participating in their preschool experience.

The suggested plan below is based on a 2½-hour session. All aspects of this plan are detailed in this section:

Activity	Approximate Time
Children arrive	
Hang up coats and schoolbags	10 minutes
Put name cards in Name Train	
Do a puzzle	10 minutes
Storytime	10 minutes
Pledge of Allegiance	
The Counter	10 minutes
Calendar	
Songs, Poems, and Fingerplay	5 minutes
Open Discussion—What's new?	5 minutes
Read Helpers' Chart	5 minutes
Readiness or cooking activity	15 minutes
Free play in classroom, painting at easel	15 minutes
Clean-up time (play song: "Whistle While You Work")	5 minutes
Outside play, indoor Music and Movement activity, or special seasonal activity	15 minutes
Milk and snack	
Sharing	15 minutes
Clean-up	5 minutes
Readiness game	5 minutes
Review day's readiness activity	5 minutes
Storytime or video	10 minutes
Get ready to go home	5 minutes

Each teacher has different gifts and talents—whether this be in music, art, dance, storytelling, and so forth. Be sure to share that special "you" with the children during your busy preschool day.

NAME TAGS

Here are two name tags you can reproduce and give to the children to wear for the first week of school. Name tags give the children a sense of belonging, as well as serve to help you learn your children's names during those first hectic days. You can either send the tags to each child when mailings go out regarding your school calendar; or you can give them to each child the first time you greet him or her. You might also make some extras to decorate the door.

─────── ROOM ARRANGEMENT AND MATERIALS ───────

The arrangement of your preschool furniture has a definite effect on the overall smooth-running of your program and the atmosphere in your classroom. For preschoolers, a room that is divided into centers gives the children a sense of security, orderliness, and direction. Dividing the room into centers also separates activities so that the children are able to concentrate on and enjoy each area. Although the areas should be well-defined, room to walk easily from one area to another must be maintained. Shelves for blocks, manipulatives, and books should be at an easily accessible height for the children. Plan for safe use of all preschool equipment and supplies.

See the illustration of a suggested room arrangement (on page 6) to help you set up your own room.

Buy quality materials in the quantity and selection your budget will permit; then, each year add to your collection. You need *not* have every item listed to run a successful program.

General Room Furnishings

Tables (kidney-shaped and round)	Film screen
Easel	Projector
Chairs	TV/VCR
Cubbies	Duplicating machine
Carpeting or a rug	First aid kit
Slide	Teacher's desk and chair
Bulletin board	File cabinet
Storage boxes and cabinets	Balance beam
Paper cutter	

Block Area

Beginning set of 80 to 100 blocks in assorted sizes (choose smoothly sanded hardwood blocks)	Wood cars and trucks
	Wood people and animals

Manipulatives

Wood puzzles	Rubber stamps and pads
Pegboards and pegs	Large floor puzzles
Large wood beads and strings	Stacking cubes
Matching cards	Plastic interlocking building blocks
Sequence cards	Sewing cards and lacing
Attribute shapes	
Magnetic number fishing set	

Name Tag

Name Tag

Suggested Room Arrangement

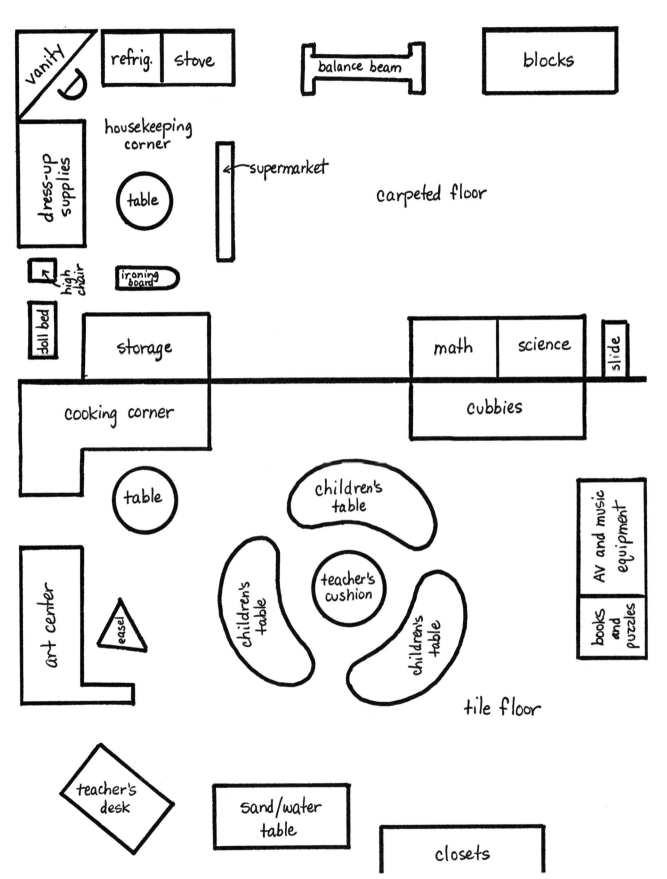

Dramatic Play

Dress-up clothes
Toy phone
Stove
Sink
Refrigerator
Ironing board and iron
Doll with clothes
Doll's bed

Highchair
Small table and two chairs
Broom
Utensils and dish set
Pots and pans
Artificial foods
Baby bottle
Cash register with play money

Music and Movement

Record or tape player
Records or tapes

Instruments (triangles, drums, maracas, rhythm sticks, cymbals, bells, piano)

Math

Counting blocks
Calendar
Number rods
Sorting/counting items

Floor hopscotch numbers
Tactile number blockboard
Counting box
Number pegboard

Sand and Water Play

Sand/water table with cover
Sand
Sand mill
Shovels
Pails
Molds

Sieves
Cups and containers
Sink and float objects
Water pump
Boats
Rubber duck

Science

Weatherboard
Magnifying glasses
Magnets
Food colorings
Color paddles

Root garden, soil, seeds
Sink and float objects
Globe
Measuring cups
Collection of seeds, rocks, leaves, shells

Art

Construction paper
Markers
Crayons

Newsprint
Tracing paper
Old magazines

Safety scissors
Hole puncher
Glue
Tape
Pencils
Tempera paints
Brushes
Smocks

Clay, clay hammers, mats
Colored tissue paper
Oaktag
Chalkboards and colored chalk
Glitter
Pompons
Sponges

Outdoor Play

Hula hoops
Balls
Paddles
Climber, slide, swings
Bean bags
High steppers

Nerf™ ball and bat
Jumping balls
Tricycles
Tumbling mats
Ring toss

COOKING IN THE CLASSROOM

Included in each monthly section are recipes for you and your children to use in the room. Cooking can be an exciting addition to your curriculum that will benefit your children in many ways.

If you don't have kitchen facilities available, set aside a corner of your room as the Kitchen Center. If your budget doesn't permit you to buy the needed equipment to stock the kitchen, you might ask parents to donate or lend some of the needed equipment. Many parents have some of these items at home that they don't use, or have duplicates, and are very happy to contribute them to your program.

You need the following basic kitchen equipment:

Toaster oven
Hot plate
Blender
Mixer
Variety of pots and pans
Mixing bowls
Cupcake tins
Strainer
Grater
Rolling pin

Paring knife
Mixing spoon
Cookie sheet
Wind-up timer
Measuring cups
Measuring spoons
Pot holders
Can opener
Set of strong, serrated plastic
    knives for children to use

While participating in these cooking experiences, your children will be developing a cooking vocabulary; increasing math concepts by measuring, counting and dividing;

and improving their fine motor and eye-hand coordination skills through peeling, cutting and mixing. They will be learning to follow directions, to taste new foods, and to clean up. Before starting any cooking project, it is very important to review the safety measures that accompany the particular recipe as well as general precautions regarding cooking and baking in general. Emphasize that the children are never to cook at school or at home without an adult. The use of the stove and the small electrical appliances are for adult use only.

HELPERS' CHART

Preschoolers love to help out. An interesting *Helpers' Chart* is a colorful room decoration and a detail-awareness skill builder. It also helps teach responsibility. Use as many real objects as possible to make your chart three-dimensional, motivating, and easy for your children to "read." Staple these objects to a corkboard or tape them onto a large sheet of oaktag.

Write the children's names on index cards and thumbtack the names under the jobs. Change the names to different jobs each week. The children's curiosity about what job they will have each week goes far in providing an incentive for them to recognize their names.

You can make an interesting activity out of changing the children's names to a new job. As you remove each name, say the name and encourage the children to say it along with you. You can say, "Amy is not going to be the Straw Person, Rob is not going to be . . ." After you have removed all the name cards, put the top card on the bottom of the pile. As you put a different name under each symbol, you can say, "Our new Milk Person's name starts with a J" (make the J sound), then say the name. Although many preschoolers are not ready to hear phonetic sounds, it gives them the idea that letters do have sounds.

"THE COUNTER"

You can add "The Counter" to your Helpers' chart. This child's job is to count the children in the class. While the class is seated, "The Counter" counts the children by touching each child's shoulder. "The Counter" then selects the proper numeral card and places it in the correct pocket. At first, "The Counter" will need help in counting and selecting the numeral. Each day, "The Counter" starts from one and counts up to the needed numeral.

NAME TRAIN

Here's a perky room decoration that's simple to make and can serve as a daily skill builder. When made, the train cars will have pockets your children can put their Name Cards into when they arrive each day for preschool. The train cars should be taped on the walls around your room. As the children arrive for class, they find their Name Card and put it in a train car pocket.

Doing this daily sets an orderly entrance atmosphere for the children. It's also a very effective way for children to begin to recognize both their names and those

of their classmates. The children quickly begin to realize that the children's cards that are not in the train are absent. They can count the cards remaining and you can write the numeral on the blackboard each day. When all the children are present, it's a good opportunity to introduce the concept of "zero." For a casual phonics alphabet and letter recognition lesson, you can hold up the absent children's name cards, point out the first letter, and make the sound while the children try to guess the name. Finally, the children's names in the train give them a sense of belonging and a feeling that this "is *my* preschool room."

To make the train cars, you need: one 12″ x 18″ sheet of colored construction paper for each child in your class and one 4½″ x 12″ (half of a 9″ x 12″) sheet of construction paper for each child. With a small plate or large margarine lid, trace half-wheels on the 12″ x 18″ construction paper. Draw straight lines and cut as shown.

Decorate the 4½″ x 12″ piece of paper and staple it onto the 12″ x 18″ paper as shown on the following page.

Use double-faced tape to tape the train cars around the room. Connect the cars with a small strip of paper or a chalk line if the cars are taped to a chalkboard.

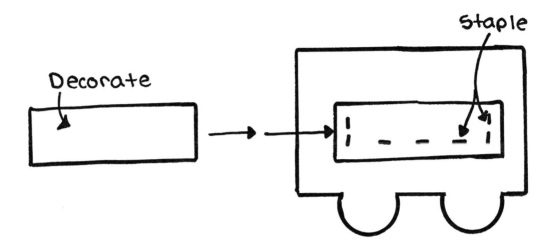

To make a name card for each child, cut a 9″ x 12″ sheet of construction paper (or oaktag for longer use) in half on the 12–inch side (you'll have two 6″ x 9″ pieces). Write the child's name towards the top of the card.

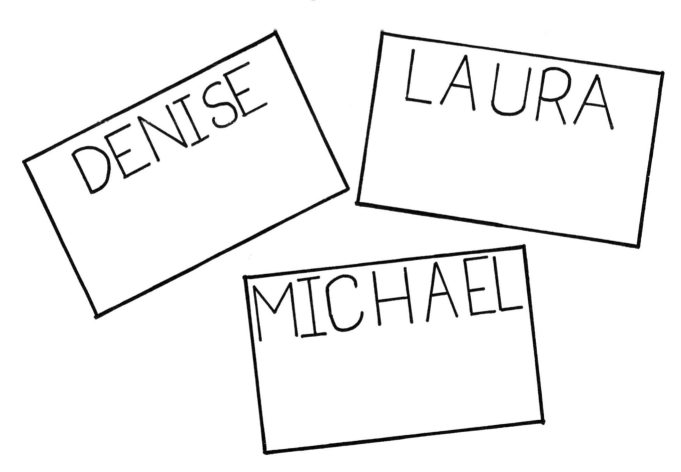

Lay all your students' cards on a table. Have the children find their own and put it in a train pocket.

In the beginning, you might put a different animal sticker on each card to help the children find their own name.

CALENDAR

A large wall calendar with Velcro™ numbers is a great tool for teaching numeral recognition, concrete counting, and day-of-the-week and month awareness. Keep all the calendar numbers in order in a small bucket. The *Calendar Person* (from the Helpers' Chart) takes the top number from the bucket and holds it up for the class to see. Then the child sticks it in the appropriate box on the calendar. After the new number is in place, have the Calendar Person point (with you) to each number, starting with number one, while the class recites the numbers. Put a holiday sticker or cutout on the special day(s) in each month, then count how many days until that holiday. On Mondays, explain that the Calendar Person has to put up three numbers—two for the weekend days when we are not in school, and one for today. Mention the name of the month each day and point out the letter it starts with.

SNACK TIME

This very popular time of the day can be a perfect opportunity to teach memory skills, concrete counting, following directions, one-to-one correspondence, orderliness, and table manners.

Have the children sit in their places at the table(s). Before you give the straws and napkins to the Straw Person and Napkin Person (from the Helpers' Chart), ask the children if they remember who the Straw Person is this week. Who is the Napkin Person?

Count the children by touching each child's shoulder (concrete) then count the appropriate number of straws and napkins aloud. Instruct your helpers to give out the straws and napkins in an orderly manner. If the milk comes to you in a milk crate, position the crate in a central spot so that the Milk Person can give out containers without getting in the way of the other Helpers.

Give instructions on how to open the milk containers. Encourage neighbors to help one another. A wicker basket with a napkin liner is a good serving basket for cookies. Be sure to include a variety of cookies, including some plain crackers such as Saltines®, Social Teas®, or Ritz® Crackers. If each parent sends in one box of cookies or other appropriate snack (raisins, popcorn, apples, cheese slices, carrot sticks) once a month, you'll have a good supply for the month. If you ask (in your initial "Beginnings" letter) for one parent a month to bring napkins instead of cookies, you'll be well supplied. For example:

Napkin List

Instead of sending in a snack with your child at the beginning of each month, please send in a family-sized package of napkins on the month indicated below. Thank you!

Amy	September
Craig	October
Michael	November
(etc.)	

On your Helpers' Chart you can indicate a Garbage Person. Roll paper into a cylinder and tape it closed to form a garbage can. Crunch up some scrap paper, insert it into the garbage can, and tape to the chart. The Garbage Person slides the room's garbage can around from one child to the next. Each child gently puts in his or her used napkin, straw and straw paper, and empty milk container. If the container has leftover milk in it, have the children either leave it on the table for you to dispose of later, or have them close the front of the container (back to its original position) and carefully place it in the garbage can. Having the children walk to a sink to empty remaining milk often encourages them to leave some!

SHARING

Also known as "Show and Tell," sharing is a traditionally popular activity among young children. Encouraging children to share the experience behind an item they are showing adds interest and language skill development to this activity. It also teaches children to listen. Send home a "Sharing" dates list (see the sample) so you can arrange to have only two sharers a day. In this way, the audience will not become restless. Encourage the audience to say "thank you for sharing" or to clap for each presenter. A good time to do sharing is at milk and snack time.

Sharing Dates

Date	Name	Name
September 10	Douglas	Lauren
September 11	Dayle	Paige

STORYTIME

Storytime is a very special part of the preschool day. The atmosphere at storytime should be calm and controlled. Polite, appropriate storytime behavior should always be complimented so that children know what is expected of them at this special time of the day. You might begin by sitting in a circle on the rug. A nice way to set up an even circle is for you and the children to hold hands in a circle and sing the following song to the tune of "Here We Go 'Round the Mulberry Bush," and then stop, drop hands, and sit down:

Here we go 'round at Storytime,
At Storytime,
At Storytime.
Here we go 'round at Storytime
On every preschool morning (afternoon).

If you prefer to have the children sit on the floor in front of you, be sure to sit on a small chair so that the book and the children are not too far apart.

During the story, stop and ask for the children's impressions, opinions, or comments. You can draw out your quieter preschoolers by asking them some simple questions about the stories, such as "Do you think baby brother wants to go to school, too?" or "What's happening at school to make him want to go?"

As your days of preschool progress, it is good to refer back to stories you have already read that were particularly appropriate to your social and moral objectives. Also, to expand upon the story, you can have the children act out some interesting and funny situations described in the books. Have a few children be the actors and actresses while the other children are the audience. The children will enjoy play-acting some of the simple stories listed in each month's section of Storytime. For instance, with the "September Storytime" book *School,* your children will enjoy acting out the part of the mother taking her hesitant child to school. In *Crazy Clothes,* they'll enjoy talking their clothes into behaving. Let the children make up their own words. Ask them, "If you were the mommy (daddy), what would you say to your child who didn't want to go to preschool?" Or, "What would you tell your shirt if it wouldn't cooperate with you?"

Music and movement can also enhance and expand upon your stories. Try putting on a record with a soft-sounding tone and have the children crawl around as quiet baby brother mouse. Or set up a balance beam and play some circus music so that the children can pretend to be tightrope walkers like the one you read about in *The Nock Family Circus.*

Another idea which brings Storytime into your curriculum is to have the children paint some simple symbol from each story at the easel.

LETTER TO PARENTS

Communication with parents is vital to the effective building of your program. Included in each monthly section is a letter called *Beginnings* aimed at informing parents about what's going on in preschool. You can add your own personal messages, comments, and dates to remember, or make copies of the letters and use them exactly as they appear.

Letting parents know that your program is organized, meaningful, and caring will enhance parent/teacher relationships. With the monthly "Beginnings" information at hand, parents are likely to become more active participants in their children's education. They will be extending your lessons and efforts into home conversations and other related activities. This positive link with your children's parents can be of great value when you need their help for a special project or activity. So communicate—send home "Beginnings" every month.

BIRTHDAY CROWN

Make copies of the "Birthday Crown" so that you'll have a supply on hand. Have the birthday child color a birthday crown and cut it out, then staple it onto a band to fit the child's head. Set aside a special time for the birthday child to wear the crown and for the class to sing "Happy Birthday." Include the end phrase "How old are you now," allowing the birthday child to state his or her new age at the end of the song. Then have the class, in unison, give a big clap for each year. Let the birthday child distribute a special treat to the class. Most preschoolers' parents enjoy sending in cupcakes, lollipops, or other special treats for their child to give out to classmates. You can mention each child's birthday in the monthly "Beginnings" letter to parents.

Summer birthdays can be celebrated in June, either each on a separate day, or group them for a gala *summer birthdays party.* For the latter, you could ask each birthday child's parents to bring in a different treat.

Birthday Crown

A Preschool Birthday

Welcome to September!

Preschoolers come to school with a variety of emotions and energies. They need to feel secure and safe in this environment. Your positive attitude and smile will go a long way in assuring them that you are competent and caring. Most preschoolers are initially torn between wanting to stay home and wanting to participate in school. When they see what great fun preschool can be, they'll be anxious for each new day to begin!

Beginnings

SEPTEMBER

Dear Parents:

Welcome!
Psychologists and educators agree that during the years between birth and five years old, children develop, learn, and grow more than they ever will again during any other period of their lives. To capitalize on these vital years, your child's preschool experience has been carefully planned.

Our preschool program is designed to develop basic concepts, attitudes, and skills, as well as to capitalize on each child's propensity to create. At all times the development of your child's self-esteem and confidence is of paramount importance. To build a broad foundation for your child's success as a student, we will be focusing upon these essential early childhood skills:

Socialization	*Shape and numeral recognition*
Language development	*Direction following*
Eye-hand coordination	*Perceptual discrimination*
Manual dexterity	*Listening*
Small muscle control	*Spatial relationships*
Conceptual development	*Color awareness*

During this first month of school the children will get to know one another, and we will establish some school routines and rules.

Our readiness activities will mark our entry into the wonderful world of colors, shapes, numbers, and letters. We will be singing, painting, coloring, and playing.

I look forward to sharing a great year with your child!

Sincerely,

_____ SEPTEMBER STORYTIME _____

The following books will help your new preschoolers realize that they're not alone in feeling "jitters" when beginning school.

School by EMILY ARNOLD McCULLY (Harper & Row)

A beautifully illustrated, wordless book about a mouse family's helter-skelter first morning of school. After all the school-aged mice are off to school, baby brother, left in the all-too-quiet house with Momma Mouse, sneaks off to see what school is all about.

Timothy Goes to School by ROSEMARY WELLS (Dial Press)

Timothy's first days of school are made unpleasant by Claude who does everything right. Then Timothy meets Violet. Their friendship helps Timothy see school and Claude in a new light.

First Day of School by KIM JACKSON (Troll Associates)

Cindy is excited about her new clothes and the first day of school. When she arrives at school with her mother, she is taken aback by the size of the school, the halls, and her teacher. Making a friend changes her fear to happiness.

Crazy Clothes by NIKI YEKTAI (Bradbury Press)

Getting dressed by oneself is a skill preschoolers all struggle with. Patrick attempts to tame his crazy clothes and show Mommy he is old enough to dress himself. Your children will laugh with and cheer for Patrick.

Will I Have a Friend? by MIRIAM COHEN (E. M. Hale & Co.)

Pa takes Jim to school for the first time. Jim's only concern is if he can make a friend at school. Things do not look too good until Jim meets Paul, a boy with similar interests. The whole socialization process improves from then on.

Starting School by KATE PETTY AND LISA KOPPER (Aladdin Books Ltd., Franklin Watts)

Sam's mom and younger sister walk him to school for his first day of school. Sam is apprehensive but soon lets go of mom and joins in the fun. He paints, plays, shares, helps, works, and listens at storytime. All the way home, Sam sings the new song he has just learned in school.

The next two books are delightful stories to share with your students. These stories can also lead to many other activities in different subject areas.

The Gingerbread Boy by PAUL GALDONE (Houghton Mifflin)

This is a classic—beautifully illustrated and worded. Throughout the story the gingerbread boy sings his boastful song: "Run, run, run as fast as you can, you can't catch me, I'm the gingerbread boy." He meets a host of hungry characters on his journey, none of whom are able to catch him. As fate would have it, he meets up with the sly fox and goes the way of every little gingerbread boy that ever came out of an oven.

Make the gingerbread boy projects described under "Readiness Activities for September."

The Nock Family Circus by URSULA HUBER (Atheneum House, Inc.)

This book is about a real circus family. It tells the tale of circus life with all its joys and its frustrations. Celestino Piatti's award-winning illustrations of the clowns, tightrope walkers, and circus animals are delightful!

———— READINESS ACTIVITIES FOR SEPTEMBER ————

Me in Preschool

Make a copy of the "Me in Preschool" worksheet for each child. Then say, "We are all different and very special. With your markers or crayons, make your face, ears, and hair. Color your clothes, too. Use a big mirror to look at your face. What color are your eyes? What color is your hair? Find those colors in your crayon or marker box. Look at your neighbors' eyes and hair colors. Who has short hair? Who has long hair? What colors are in your clothes today?"

Mosaic Apple

Apples make a great finger-food snack. Bring in a few different kinds and sizes of apples, such as Golden, Granny Smith, and Red Delicious. Let the children feel their skins. Which apple has the smoothest skin? Which is the shiniest? The smallest? The largest? Name the colors. Cut open the apples and show the seeds to the children. Ask them why the apple makes seeds. Have a taste-testing party. Cut up the apples and give each child a small piece of each apple. Ask them, "Which is the sweetest? The juiciest? Which one do you like best?"

Now have your children make this apple mosaic. Make a copy of the "Mosaic Apple" worksheet for each child. Then say, "Decide which color apple you like best. With that color crayon or marker, color the rectangle at the bottom of the page. Cut out the rectangle, then cut on all the small lines so that you have a lot of little squares. Put a small drop of glue on the X on the apple. Lay on one small square. Continue doing this all the way around the apple. Then color the apple's leaf green."

Pussy Willows

Bring in a pussy willow branch or show a picture of one. Tell the children that the small knobs on the branches are called *catkins,* because they are soft and fuzzy like a little pussy cat.

Make a copy of the pussy willow worksheet for each child. Then say, "With your crayons or markers, color the pussy willow branches brown and the leaves green. Go over the words *pussy willow* with your crayon or marker. In a small cup, put a shallow amount of white paint, tinted with a drop of yellow paint. Dip the tip of your index finger or a cotton swab into the white paint and press down on the side of one of the branches. Continue until you cover both sides of each branch with catkins."

Clay or Salt Dough Gingerbread Boy or Girl

Read the story *The Gingerbread Boy* (see "September Storytime") and have the children learn this little song: "Run, run, run, as fast as you can; you can't catch me, I'm the gingerbread boy;" then help the children make gingerbread boys and girls from clay or salt dough. Use a dull pencil to make impressions in the figures for eyes, nose, mouth, and buttons. You can air-dry the salt dough and let each child take home his or her own gingerbread figure.

SALT DOUGH RECIPE: Mix together in a large bowl 4 cups flour and 1 cup salt. While stirring, add approximately 1½ cups water and 1 tablespoon oil. Knead for about five minutes. The clay will keep a week or so in a tightly closed plastic bag in the refrigerator. If it becomes gummy, leave it at room temperature and add a bit more flour.

A Paper Gingerbread Boy or Girl

Using the salt dough gingerbread figure and a sheet of paper, have each child go around the outside line of the figure with a black marker. Then color in the eyes, nose, and mouth with the black marker. Lightly color the gingerbread figure with brown crayon, and cut the figure out. Don't let it run away! (See the September recipe for gingerbread cookies to enjoy the delicious figures!)

The Gingerbread Boy's Raisins

Make a copy of the "Count the Raisins" worksheet for each student. Say, "Count the number of raisins on each gingerbread boy. Go over each numeral on the spoon. Then color the gingerbread boys light brown."

Community Helper—Animal Shelter Worker

Call your local ASPCA or animal shelter and ask if your class could visit, or if they have a speaker who can come to the classroom. Having a short talk on the proper way to treat household dogs and cats, as well as animals encountered on the street, could go a long way toward preventing bites and scratches.

Make a copy of the "C Is for Cat" worksheet for each child. Then say, "There are many sizes and types of cats. Their colorings and markings are very different from one another. Color this friendly cat. Show how you would gently pet the cat if it were real."

A Paper Cat or Dog

Make a copy of "A Paper Cat or Dog" worksheet for each child. Then say, "Cut out these shapes. Try making a dog or cat from the shapes. Draw a face and whiskers on the square. Then use your imagination to decorate your cat or dog." Here is one example of how a cat might look.

Cute-as-a-Button Needs Ears

Make a copy of the "Cute-as-a-Button" worksheet for each child. Say, "The bunny's name is 'Button.' But he needs ears! Follow the numbers from one to eight. Now color Button and his bow so that he looks as 'cute as a button.' "

Seeds, Seeds

Make a copy of the "Seeds, Seeds" worksheet for each child. Then say, "These fruits make good nutritional snacks. Each of these fruits makes seeds so that more fruit can grow. How many seeds are in each of these fruits? Do you know the names of these fruits? Have you tasted any of these fruits at home? Which is your favorite fruit? The next time you eat one of these fruits, try to save the seeds and bring them to class. Now, color the three fruits. Trace over the numerals."

Observe Growth

Examine a number of different kinds of seeds. Note the different sizes, shapes, and colors of the seeds. Help the children make a seed chart of the different seeds they have, then give the children a small pile of seeds to sort and match to the chart.

Explain that inside every seed is a little root and a little sprout. The root goes down into the soil and the sprout heads up to the light to form the plant.

Place some lima beans on a moist sponge in a shallow dish. Cover with plastic wrap and keep warm for one or two days. Notice how the plant inside begins to grow. Point out the root and the sprout.

Now plant some of the beans in a glass filled with soil. Plant the beans close to side of the glass. Check daily for growth. Plant a sprouted bean upside down. Notice how the stem will curve upward and the root will bend downward within a few days.

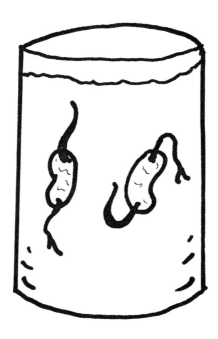

Plants Need Light

To demonstrate how plants naturally turn toward the light, place a young sprouted seedling on the windowsill. As the plant grows, it will bend toward the light. After showing this bending to the children, turn the plant around 90°. The children will be able to observe that the plant again begins to bend toward the light.

Plants Need Water

Discuss the plant's need for water as well as light with the children. Place two similar seedlings on the windowsill. Water one regularly. Withhold water from the other. What happens?

Do the celery experiment. Fill a jar with water and place a stalk of celery, leaves up, in the water. (Cut about a half-inch off the bottom of the stalk before placing it in the water.) Add four to six drops of red or blue food coloring to the water. Observe for several days. What happens?

We All Need Water

To continue further development of the children's awareness and appreciation of water, ask the children to think of ways to use water aside from watering plants. Some suggestions are:

for drinking

for washing clothes

for bathing

for cooking

for making ice cubes

for swimming

for making tea and coffee

for pets

for making powdered fruit drinks

for boating

for watercolors

for a fish tank

Do some water activities with your children:

- Make a gelatin dessert. Have the children observe the boiling water and steam.
- Mix water with a powdered fruit drink mix. Have the children observe the measuring of the water and the dissolving of the powder.
- Add food color to glasses of water. Have the children observe the mixing of the two colors to make a new color.
- Wet a piece of construction paper. Put it on a sunny windowsill and have the children observe the evaporation of water over a period of time.
- Make ice cubes. Then watch them melt.
- Paint with watercolors and compare the result to a tempera painting.
- Use water to cook some vegetables. Compare how they look and taste with their raw counterparts.
- Mix water with some dry sand and observe the differences between the two. Form the wet sand into some simple shapes. Try doing it with dry sand.

• Do some sink/float experiments in a tub of water. Allow the children to experiment on their own.

A September Tree

Make a copy of "A September Tree" worksheet for each child. Then say, "What color are the leaves on the trees around the school now? Are they still green? After looking at a real tree, color this tree and its leaves to match the tree you saw. Then cut out all the boxes of leaves and glue the leaves onto the tree."

A Is for Apple

Jonathan Chapman ("Johnny Appleseed") planted apple seeds wherever he found good soil. His apple trees were welcomed by the early settlers in America. Apple trees now grow everywhere in the United States except in the very hot southwest.

Make a copy of the "A Is for Apple" worksheet for each child. Then say, "There are many different kinds and colors of apples. Color these three apples by looking at the clue that is the same color as the apple."

My Number Book

Make a copy of the "My Number Book" worksheet for each child. Say, "Trace each numeral and color the apples. Cut the pages apart. Put the pages in order and staple them together in the left-hand corner. Then 'read' the book. Touch each apple as you count it."

About Me

Make a copy of the "About Me" worksheet for each child. Say, "A very special YOU comes with a name, an address, a phone number—and now a school! Draw your face in the circle. Color the house, the telephone, and the school."

A "Me" Poster

This is a good decoration for your classroom during Open School Week. Have the children bring in baby pictures or any other mementoes their parents have saved throughout the years. Also ask for some recent photos. Make a poster of these objects for each child. You can also help the children draw simple pictures of things they like, or just list them ("I like red balloons, ice cream, flowers . . .").

Button's Number Blocks

If you have blocks with numbers on them, you can play many games with your children. Line up the blocks in order. Touch and count them. Then take three out and hand them to three different children, telling them their number. Read the numbers left in the line and instruct the children to come up with their block when you get to the space where it belongs. You might also write numbers on small pieces of paper and tape them to regular wooden blocks.

Make a copy of "Button's Number Blocks" worksheet for each child. Say, "Button didn't have time to put all the number blocks back on the shelf. Will you help Button? Color all the blocks with light-colored crayons. Then cut out the number blocks at the bottom of the page and glue them where they belong."

What's Missing?

This is a visual memory game. Have the children sit in a large circle. Put three familiar items on the floor, and mention the name of each item. Then have the children repeat the names of the items as you point to each one. Cover the three items with a cloth. Move your hand under the cloth and take one item away as you take the cloth off the items. The "missing" item remains inside the cloth, hidden. Ask, "What's missing?" Repeat this activity, adding more items as the students become more proficient.

SHAPE RECOGNITION

The recognition of basic shapes is an important prereading skill. If children become familiar with the basic shapes, they will be able to recognize alphabet letter shapes more easily.

Attribute blocks (plastic geometric shapes in varying colors, sizes, and thicknesses) can be handled by the children so that they can "feel" the shapes. The children can sort the shapes by their various attributes.

The rectangles and squares in the following projects can be quickly and easily cut if you use a paper cutter and two or three sheets of construction paper at a time. With practice, you can also cut rectangle strips into triangles on the paper cutter.

Fall Rectangle Frame

Give each child a pile of rectangles in fall colors. Discuss the names of these colors, the fall season, and the change in color that the leaves on the trees will be going through. Have the children glue the rectangles around the edge of a piece of construction paper. (Remind them that each rectangle only needs one tiny drop of glue.)

To fill the frame:

1. Have the children draw pictures of themselves, adding dots of fall colors to represent leaves falling. OR . . .

2. Have the children collect fall leaves. Press them for a few days in a magazine under some books. Glue the leaves inside the frame. (If you spray the leaves with clear acrylic, they will last beautifully.)

Shape Chain

You will need manila tags or white construction paper shapes, yarn, and markers or crayons.

Give each child a set of shapes—oval, triangle, rectangle, circle, square. Have the children color each shape a different color, or decorate them with dots and stripes. As they are coloring, have them make a pile of their shapes so that they don't get mixed up with their neighbor's shapes. When they have completed their coloring, you can punch a hole in the top of each shape and string them with yarn. If you knot each shape, they will hang separately. Have each child wear his or her shape chain home.

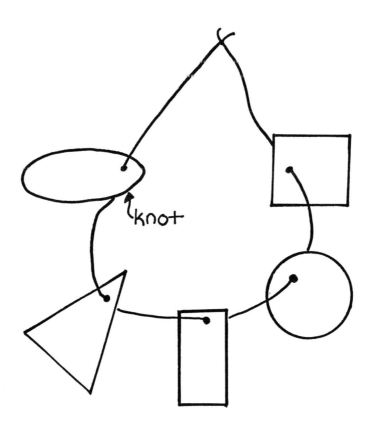

Shape Collage

You will need assorted small paper shapes, 9″ x 12″ construction paper, and glue.

This is a good activity to use to teach the proper use of glue or paste. Name the shapes for the children. Put a handful of small shapes between two children. Explain that in a shape collage they can glue the shapes anyplace on the paper, and that only a *small* drop of glue is needed to hold each shape in place.

"Shapey"

You will need 9″ x 12″ construction paper, 1 paper circle, 1 paper square, 4 paper rectangles (2 short, 2 long) and glue.

Give each child a set of the six shapes listed. Ask them to hold up and name the shape they think they could use to make a person's head, and so on. Have the children glue each piece after selecting it, and discuss its position on the 9″ x 12″ paper. After "Shapey" dries, have the children add eyes, nose, mouth, ears, and hair.

Silly Shapes

The children will find these shapes fun to make and play with. They will quickly learn their names, reinforcing shape/name concepts. Introduce each "silly shape" by using a sample you have made and have it talk to the children. Do one "silly shape" a day.

For example, "Hi, I'm Sammy. What's your name little boy? Do you know what shape I am? Well, I have to tell you something about myself. I've been going to the Circle Dancing School for three years. Do you want to see me dance? Oh, good. I'm glad you do." (Wind up the string while Sammy is sitting on the floor or table. Ask the children to say, "Sammy, please dance." Hold the string up and watch Sammy dance. The children will love it! They'll be very motivated to make a Sammy of their own to take home.)

The following shape projects are for the children to color and for you to cut. Tell the children not to use black when coloring their shapes because you will use black to make the eyes, nose, and mouth on these silly shapes.

SAMMY THE CIRCLE: Have the children color a 5″ oaktag or white construction paper circle. You can divide the circle into small sections and ask the children to color each section a different color. Cut the circle into a spiral, leaving a small circle in the middle. In this circle, draw eyes, nose, and mouth with a black marker. Punch a hole in the top of Sammy's head and string with a piece of yarn or string. If you wind up Sammy's string, he will dance.

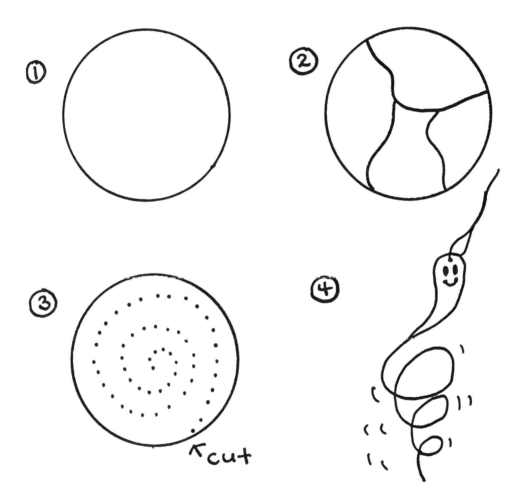

TRICKY TRIANGLE: Tricky likes to make believe she's a flamingo standing on one leg. Remember to introduce Tricky to the children as you did Sammy. Have the children color a 5″ triangle pink, or lightly use a red crayon. Cut the triangle as shown, leaving a small triangle in the center. Draw the eyes, and draw a beak in the small triangle. Punch a hole in Tricky's head and string with yarn or string. Wind up the string and watch Tricky do a flamingo dance. Introduce Tricky to Sammy. Hold one in each hand and have a dance contest!

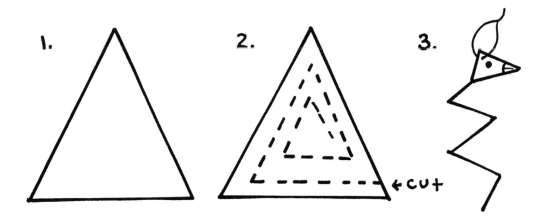

REX THE RECTANGLE: Rex is a rectangle cowboy. Using a western drawl, have Rex say hello to each child. Have the children color Rex in their favorite colors. (You can divide the rectangle into three parts to make the coloring easier.) Cut out a cowboy hat for each Rex and have the children color it brown. Cut Rex as shown. Glue on his hat and tie on a piece of string. Wind up the string to make Rex do a cowboy dance.

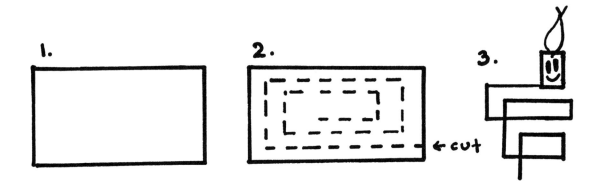

OVAL OLIVIA: Oval Olivia's name is a real challenge for the children to say. They'll love to practice saying it with you. Have Olivia compare her hair to each child's hair, saying "longer, shorter" etc., and mention each child's hair color as you go along. Olivia has long blonde hair—so have the children use yellow to color a 6″

oval. With a pencil, have them make hair lines all over Olivia. Cut the oval into a spiral, leaving a small oval in the middle. Draw eyes, nose, and mouth in this small oval. Punch a hole in Olivia's head and string with yarn or string. Wind up the string and Olivia will do the twist for you.

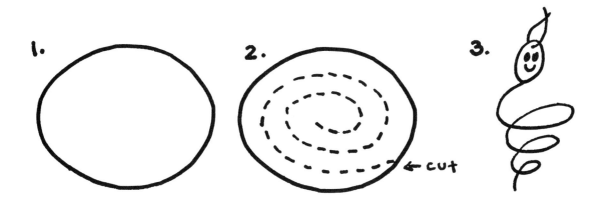

SQUIGGLE SQUARE: Although Squiggle is rather square, he's very friendly and sweet. Have Squiggle talk to the children about being kind, caring, and sharing. Have the children color a 6″ square any light color. Then have them draw squiggles all over with a dark marker or crayon. Cut as shown. Draw the eyes, nose, and mouth. Punch a hole in Squiggle's head and string with yarn or string. Wind up Squiggle and watch him do a "square" dance!

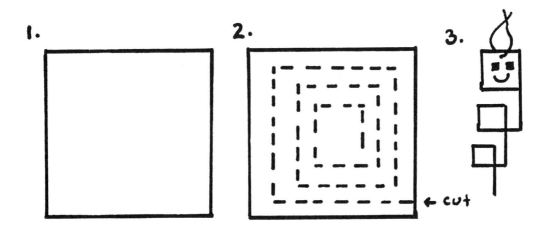

MUSIC AND MOVEMENT

The Hokeypokey

The Hokeypokey is a good song for helping to teach body parts. Identification of these parts and the appropriate use of them contributes to the enhancement of the child's self-esteem.

Stand with the children in a circle while singing. Initiate the body part and have the children imitate the action; for example, right hand, ankle, elbow, etc.

> Put your _____in.
> Put your _____out.
> Put your _____in.
> And shake it all about.
> Do the Hokeypokey. (*put both index fingers in the air*)
> And turn yourself around. (*turn around*)
> That's what it's all about! (*clap*)

End with "Put your whole self in," etc.

Did You Ever See a Lassie?

Stand with the children in a circle while singing (and swaying). When you get to "this way and that way," make a movement that the children can imitate; for example, hands on shoulders, hold one ear, etc. Remember to continue to sway. Repeat with various movements.

> Did you ever see a lassie, a lassie, a lassie?
> Did you ever see a lassie, go this way and that?
> This way and that way;
> This way and that way.
> Did you ever see a lassie go this way and that?

Preschool Fitness Album

The record *Preschool Fitness* by Pam Tims (Melody House Publishing Co., Oklahoma City, Oklahoma) provides many interesting movement situations for preschoolers. With the album's music and guidance, the children can imagine they are taking their ponies for a ride, that they are helicopters twirling in the sky, or that they are soldiers obeying a drill sergeant's commands.

SONGS, POEMS, AND FINGERPLAYS

Where Is Thumbkin?

Start with hands behind your back.

1. Where is thumbkin? Where is thumbkin? Here I am.
   Here I am.

How are you this morning? Very well, I thank you. Run and hide. Run and hide.

Move hands behind your back to end each verse.
2. Where is pointer?
3. Where is tall one?
4. Where is ringer?
5. Where is pinkie?

Ten Fingers

Show all ten fingers by holding your hands up. Then suit the rest of the motions to the words:

> I have ten little fingers,
> They all belong to me.
> I can make them do things,
> Would you like to see?
>
> I can shut them up tight,
> Or open them wide.
> I can put them all together,
> Or make them all hide.
>
> I can make them jump high,
> I can make them jump low.
> I can fold them quietly,
> And hold them just so.

My Turtle

> This is my turtle. (*make fist, extend thumb*)
> He lives in a shell. (*hide thumb in fist*)
> He likes his home very well.
> He pokes his head out when he wants to eat. (*extend thumb*)
> And he pulls it back in when he wants to sleep. (*hide thumb in fist*)

Little Bird

> I saw a little bird go hop, hop, hop.
> I told the little bird to stop, stop, stop.
> I went to the window to say, "How do you do?"
> It wagged its little tail and away it flew.

FROM BUTTON'S COUNTRY KITCHEN

Gingerbread Cookies

1½ sticks of soft margarine	¼ teaspoon ground cloves
½ cup sugar	1 egg
2 teaspoons ground ginger	¾ cup molasses
½ teaspoon salt	3 cups all-purpose flour
1 teaspoon cinnamon	1 teaspoon baking soda

Preheat the oven to 350°F. Grease a cookie sheet. Mix all ingredients together in a large bowl. Roll out the dough on a floured surface to an ⅛″ thickness. Cut the gingerbread figures with a cookie cutter. Decorate with raisins. Bake on the cookie sheet for about 8 minutes.

Applesauce

You will need about a pound of apples for every cup of applesauce you want to make. MacIntosh apples are great for applesauce, although you can use any kind.

Wash and core the apples but do not peel them. Cut them into pieces. Put the apples in a pot with a little water, cook slowly and stir. When the apples become soft, you can mash them with a potato masher or put them in a blender. Pour into individual cups and sprinkle with cinnamon or nutmeg.

VIDEOS FOR SEPTEMBER

Three Richard Scarry Animal Nursery Tales (Western Publishing Co., Racine, WI 1985)

Included are "The Gingerbread Man," "Goldilocks and the Three Bears," and "The Three Little Pigs."

In "The Gingerbread Man," the gingerbread man comes alive, jumps off Helga's baking pan, and begins a journey through the countryside. The gingerbread man's frisky romp will delight your little ones.

Use this 30-minute tape with September's gingerbread projects and book.

Little Toad to the Rescue (A Golden Book Video, Western Publishing Co., Racine, WI 1985)

Like "The Little Engine Who Could," Toad accomplishes his goal by using steadfast determination. While helping Little Toad, Toad encounters danger, adventure, and new friends. Included are "The Pokey Little Puppy" and "The Patchwork Blanket." Approximate running time: 30 minutes.

WORKSHEETS FOR SEPTEMBER

The following worksheets are referred to in this month's readiness activities.

Me in Preschool

Mosaic Apple

Pussy Willow

Count the Raisins

C is for Cat

A Paper Cat or Dog

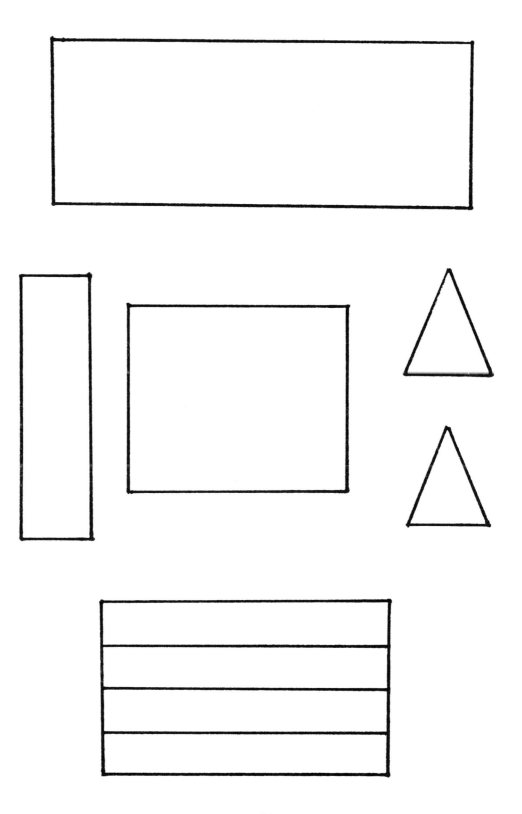

Cute-As-A-Button

45

Seeds, Seeds

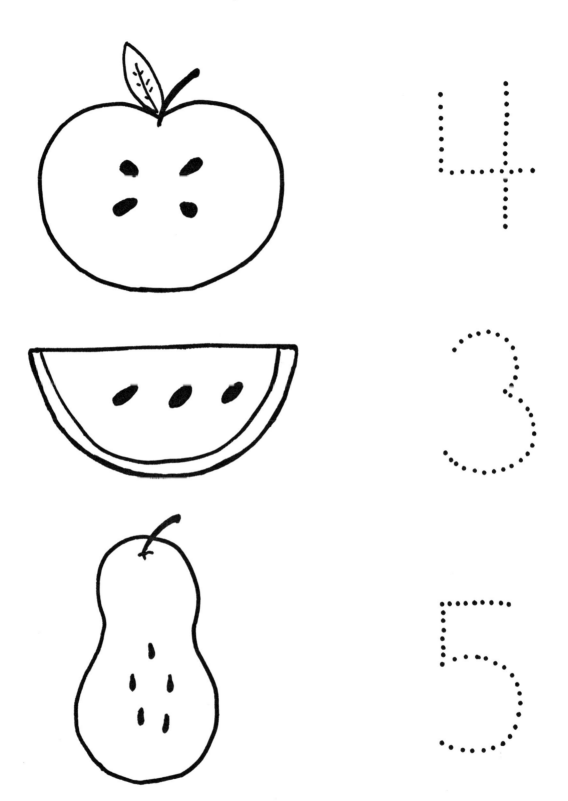

A September Tree

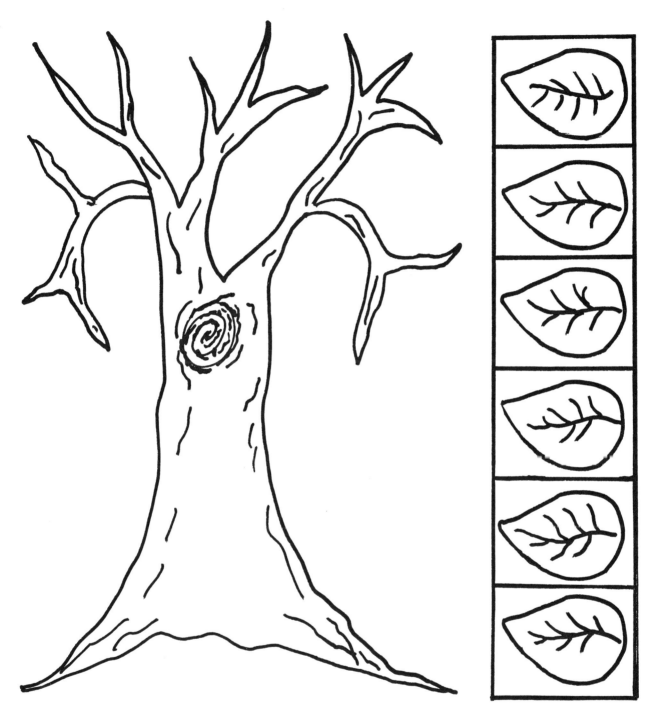

A Is for Apple

MY NUMBER BOOK

1

2

3

4

5

49

About Me

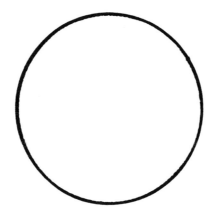

My name is _____

_____

I live at _____

_____

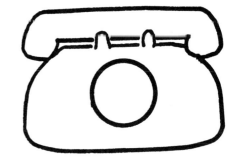

My telephone number is

_____

I go to _____
(name of school)

Button's Number Blocks

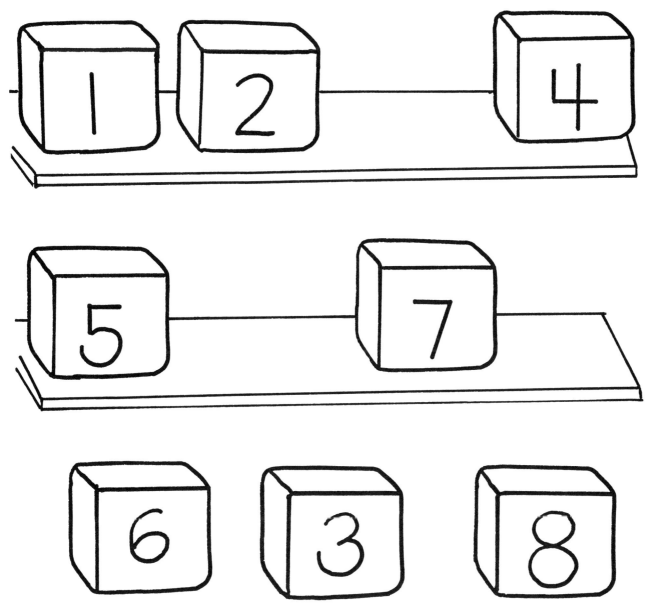

October — The Bewitching Month

Preschoolers delight in this magical month. The leaves change colors, the breeze is gusty, and you can almost smell Halloween coming. Capitalize on your children's enthusiasm by using readiness projects related to fall's color "magic" and Halloween's mystery.

Beginnings

Dear Parents:

    October is here! September has flown by in class. It was such a busy month. We all got to know each other, explored the classroom and our outside surroundings.

    This month we will be observing the wonders of nature and anticipating the thrill of Halloween. We will be reading stories connected to the season and this month's holiday.

    I invite you to join in our fun and learning by appreciating and discussing the projects your child brings home.

    Hope you have a "boooo—tiful" month!

Sincerely,

_____

OCTOBER STORYTIME

The following books will provide your preschoolers with a variety of stories about the season.

The Berenstain Bears and Too Much Junk Food by STAN AND JAN BERENSTAIN (Random House)

Brother and Sister Bear—as well as Papa Bear—have been eating too much junk food and getting too chubby. Mama Bear takes the family to the supermarket to pick out nutritious snacks. Dr. Grizzly sees the cubs and Papa picking out candy. The doctor decides the family needs to learn about their bodies and nutrition, so she presents a convincing lesson.

This book helps initiate a good lesson in nutrition. You can use your plastic fruits and veggies from the housekeeping corner to teach the naming of these healthy foods. If there is a fruit and vegetable store nearby, take your plastic food there and see if the children can find the "real" versions. (Be sure to ask the store owner's permission first!)

You can also ask each child's parent to send in a different fruit or vegetable so that you can have a "Good for You" tasting day in class.

The Very Busy Spider by ERIC CARLE (Philomel Books)

Early one morning, a little spider begins to spin her web on a fence post. The farm animals try to divert her from her work. She finally gets a chance to show that her web is not only very beautiful but also very useful. This is a multisensory book; the children can feel as well as see the web as it grows.

Shaggy Dog's Halloween by DONALD CHARLES (Children's Press)

This is a bright and perky book that details Shaggy Dog's search for a Halloween costume. The pictures provide a basis for discussions about scary Halloween costumes and decorations. In the story, Shaggy makes a paper bag mask and goes off to a party.

Paper bag masks are fun and easy to make. First, mark the eyes on a bag, cut out the eye holes, and then let the children decorate their paper bag masks.

Popcorn by FRANK ASCH (Parents/Magazine Press)

When Mama and Papa go out, Sam the bear decides to have a Halloween party. Each of his guests brings popcorn for a snack. The young bears pour all the popcorn into a big pot. When it pops, it fills the entire house. To get rid of the popcorn, all the bears eat until they are stuffed—and sick. When Sam's parents come home, they give him a present—popcorn!

Make some popcorn in class and discuss how much is enough to eat. You can have a "which bowl has more" lesson. Let the children take handfuls of popcorn and count how many pieces of popcorn each has.

That Terrible Halloween Night by JAMES STEVENSON (Greenwillow Books)

When children's efforts to scare Grandpa fail, Grandpa tells his grandchildren about the dreadful Halloween night that turned him into an old man.

Discuss the real way people "get older" with the children and encourage them to talk about the older people they know.

Joey the Jack-o'-Lantern by JANET CRAIG (Troll Associates)

Joey is a very pleasant looking jack-o'-lantern that tries his unsuccessful best to look scary for Halloween night. Finally, Willie Witch comes to his rescue and Joey is turned into the scariest and happiest jack-o'-lantern ever on Halloween night. The book has wonderful illustrations.

This book can be a good opener for any of the jack-o'-lantern activities.

The Biggest Pumpkin Ever by STEVEN KROLL (Scholastic)

This is a story about cooperation and friendship. Two mice fall in love with the same pumpkin. They each nurture it, one by day and one by night, and plan for the pumpkin's future. When the mice discover each other, they work out a deal that pleases everyone.

Read this book to the children before visiting a pumpkin farm (if possible) or a food store display. Look for the biggest pumpkin and the smallest pumpkin.

Other books about growing seeds and plants are *The Carrot and Other Root Vegetables* by Millicent Selsam (William Morrow and Co.), *Eric Plants a Garden* by Jean Hudlow (Albert Whitman and Co.), *Plant Fun* by Anita Holmes Soucie (Four Winds Press), *How a Seed Grows* by Helen J. Jordan (Thomas Crowell Co.), *A Seed Is a Promise* by Claire Merrill (Scholastic Book Services), and *A Crack in the Pavement* by Ruth Howell (Antheneum).

Chatty Chipmunk's Nutty Day by SUZANNE GRUBER (Troll Associates)

This is a nice simple story to complement your discussions about the fall season. Chatty's love for acorns prompts his search for a safe storage space.

Read this story to the children before playing the "Nut Hunt" game.

Growing Vegetable Soup by LOIS EHLERT (Harcourt Brace Jovanovich)

This book is bursting with bright, bold, and colorful vegetables. A father and child plant vegetable seeds. They nurture them and watch them grow into a lovely vegetable garden. When the vegetables are ripe, they pick, wash, and cook them to make vegetable soup. A recipe is included.

The Little Old Lady Who Was Not Afraid of Anything by LINDA WILLIAMS (Thomas Y. Crowell)

This is a different kind of Halloween story that can open the door for discussions about "being afraid." The little old lady takes a walk in the woods on an autumn night and gets the scare of her life!

Be Nice to Spiders by MARGARET BLOY GRAHAM (Harper & Row)

This is a cute story which can go along with your Halloween spider art projects. It tells a simple story about Helen the spider who makes herself useful by trapping flies that bother animals in the zoo.

Remember to sing "The Eensy Weensy Spider" found later in this chapter.

Georgie's Halloween by ROBERT BRIGHT (Doubleday)

Georgie, a shy and gentle little ghost, ventures out on Halloween night to join the children in a party on the village green. The children are glad to see him, but the shy little ghost doesn't stay long. He scampers back to his mouse friends in the attic, who have a special surprise for him.

Read this story to the children before doing the "Let's Build a Haunted House" activity.

READINESS ACTIVITIES FOR OCTOBER

Let's Build a Haunted House

Make a copy of the "Let's Build a Haunted House" worksheet for each child. Draw this simple illustration on the chalkboard.

Then say, "Look at your worksheet and color the shapes with your crayons or markers. For variety on some of the shapes, put stripes or dots. Cut out all the shapes. Then build a house like the one on the chalkboard. Glue the shapes onto a piece of construction paper. Cut out the ghosts and glue them on and around the house."

Follow-the-Numbers Pumpkin

Make a copy of the "Follow-the-Numbers Pumpkin" worksheet for each child. Say, "Follow the numbers. Then color the pumpkin orange."

You might have the children turn this pumpkin into a pumpkin seed jack-o'-lantern. Have the children glue dried pumpkin seeds onto the pumpkin to make eyes, nose, and mouth. Help them count the number of seeds they use.

G Is for Ghost

Make a copy of the "G Is for Ghost" worksheet for each child. Then say, "The word ghost begins with G. Each ghost's first name also starts with G. Go over the G at the start of each ghost's first and last names with your pencil. Then color all the ghosts."

How Many Jack-o'-Lanterns on the Fence?

Make a copy of the "How Many Jack-o'-Lanterns on the Fence?" worksheet for each child. Then say, "Count the number of pumpkins sitting on the fence. Trace the numeral. Then color the pumpkins orange and color each fence a different color."

Carrots

Bring in a bunch of carrots for the children to feel and compare sizes. Mention that carrots grow underground, and can be eaten either raw or cooked.

Make a copy of the "Carrots" worksheet for each child. Ask the children to point to the longest carrot, the shortest carrot, the fattest carrot, and the skinniest carrot. Then let them color the carrots orange.

Pumpkin and Jack-o'-Lantern Mask

In addition to a copy of the mask worksheet for each child, you will need craft sticks, glue, and either crayons or markers. Have the children color the eyes, nose, and mouth of the jack-o'-lantern black and the rest of the face orange. Then cut out the jack-o'-lantern and have the children color the reverse side completely orange. Glue the craft stick onto each mask as shown in this illustration.

Now have your children learn the following song (sung to the tune of "I'm a Little Teapot"). Show the pumpkin side of the mask throughout the song until they reach the line "I'll be a jack-o'-lantern."

I'm a little pumpkin (*pumpkin side of mask*)
Short and stout.
I'll be a jack-o'-lantern (*reverse mask*)
If you'll cut me out.

Build a Witch

Make a copy of the "Build a Witch" worksheet for each child. Say, "Draw a witch's face and hair in the circle. Color the big triangle orange. Color the small triangle black. Color the rectangles green. Then cut out all the shapes and glue them on the dotted outline where they belong."

Smiley and Sad

Make a copy of the "Smiley and Sad" worksheet for each child. Have the children count the number of smiling figures (pumpkins, cats, ghosts) in each row. Then have the children go over the numeral and color all the smiling figures.

When the children are finished with the worksheet, ask them to talk about the times they feel "smiley" and sad.

Spiders, Spiders

Make a copy of the "Spiders, Spiders" worksheet for each child. Ask the children how many spiders are on the web. Then say, "Color the spiders at the bottom of the worksheet with your crayon. Cut them out on the lines and glue the spiders onto the web. Now count how many spiders you have."

Remember to read *Be Nice to Spiders* (see "October Storytime") and to sing "The Eensy, Weensy Spider."

Grow Carrot Greenery

It's easy to grow greenery from carrot tops. Clip off all but an inch of carrot greens, leaving an inch of carrot. Place the carrot tops in a shallow pan with water and pebbles.

Press the greenery you've snipped off the bunch of carrots. It makes a beautiful lacey decoration for a card or gift.

Grow a Pineapple Plant

Cut off the top of a pineapple, leaving an inch of fruit on it. Plant the top in a pot of soil up to the base of the leaves. Keep the soil moist. In about six weeks, the pineapple top will grow roots and begin to sprout.

An Acorn Person

Squirrels love acorn nuts! Acorns grow on oak trees. In the fall, squirrels and other small animals gather food for the long winter ahead. Squirrels live in every part of the world except Australia. If there is an oak tree around school or your home, you're sure to see squirrels scurrying around the oak branches biting off acorns. The squirrels usually only eat the nut of the acorn, not its "cap." Collect some caps from under the mighty oaks and let the children make "acorn people" using "An Acorn Person" worksheet. Have the children color the acorns with markers and then glue on the caps to make eyes, noses, and mouths. Have the children count how many acorn caps they used.

Chlorophyll

You will need 6″ × 4½″ (half of 9″ × 12″) white construction paper, 6″ × 4½″ tracing paper, and either markers or crayons.

Chlorophyll is what makes a leaf green. (Three-, four-, and five-year-olds can say and remember the word "chlorophyll.") All summer long, the leaf is busy making chlorophyll and growing. In the fall, the leaf begins to stop making this green matter. As the green chlorophyll disappears, beautiful reds, yellows, browns, and oranges appear. These colors are always present in the green leaves, but cannot be seen in the summer because there is so much more green (chlorophyll) than other colors. Collect some green leaves and some fall-colored leaves to show to the children.

To demonstrate this phenomenon to the children, have them do the following project. On construction paper, draw the outline of a simple leaf, including its veins.

Have the children color each section of the leaf a different fall color. Then staple a piece of tracing paper over the leaf. Have the children trace around the outside of the leaf, then color the leaf green.

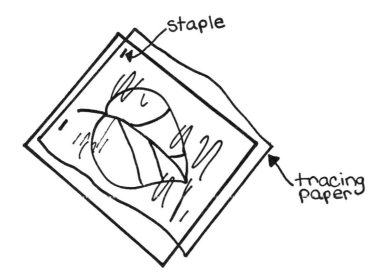

A Leaf's Veins

Collect fall leaves and show the children the leaves' veins. Explain that the veins supply the leaf with food and water to grow. (Have the children look for veins in their arms and explain how their veins carry blood to the organs and tissues to help them grow.) Let the children peel away the leaf matter from leaves to see the veins. You can squirt glue onto a piece of construction paper and let the children lay down their peeled leaves to make an interesting collage. You might also view leaves through a microscope.

Squirrel Watch

Squirrels like to spend their winters at home, preferably in the hollow of a tree. In the fall, they leave their nests in the tree tops and find a warm and cozy hole to line with twigs and leaves.

Try putting some acorns on the outside of your classroom windowsill and wait for the squirrels to come by. If you put the acorns on a piece of white paper, you may be able to see some paw prints left behind by the squirrels.

Acorns are the seeds of the oak tree. They need to be buried in the ground in order to grow into trees. Squirrels are the planters! In spring, the warm sun and rain soften the acorn shell. Cracks appear in the acorn. Two little shoots come out. One grows upward to form the trunk, and the other grows downward to form the root.

Make a copy of the "Watch the Acorn" worksheet for each child. Say, "Look at the acorn growing in the pictures below. Color the pictures. Cut the pictures apart on the solid lines and mix up the pictures. Now see if you can put them back in the correct growing order."

Nuts and More Nuts!

Bring in real acorns and a variety of other nuts for the children to handle and sort by color and size.

Make a copy of the "Nuts and More Nuts!" worksheet for each child. Then say, "Count the acorns this squirrel has gathered for the long winter to come. Trace the numerals, then color the acorn caps brown. Color the acorn nut lightly with your green crayon. How many acorns are there?"

Football Mums

Show the children a real mum (chrysanthemum) or a picture of one. (Seed and bulb catalogs have wonderful floral pictures). Note the size of football mums as compared to regular mums.

For this activity, you will need orange paint (or a mixture of red and yellow paints), soap flakes, small pieces of sponge, glue, construction paper, and crayons or markers.

In a small bowl, mix enough soap flakes into the orange paint to make it thick and paste-like. With a small piece of sponge, have the children dab the mixture onto their copy of "A Football Mum" worksheet. After the mum has dried, cut it out and glue it onto a piece of construction paper. Have the children draw a stem and leaves.

Sizes of Pumpkins

Let the children handle some real pumpkins, and put them in size order.

Make a copy of the "Sizes of Pumpkins" worksheet for each child. Then say, "Color the pumpkins and then cut them apart on the lines. Now try to put your pumpkins in order from the smallest to the largest."

The Eensy, Weensy Spider

Spiders are *not* insects. Insects have six legs, while spiders have eight legs. Insects usually have wings; spiders never do.

Make a copy of "The Eensy, Weensy Spider" worksheet for each child. Say, "With your black marker or crayon, draw eight legs on this spider. Spiders can be green, yellow, red, brown, grey, or black. Pick your favorite color or colors and fill in this spider."

Now sing "The Eensy Weensy Spider" with the children, using the finger and hand motions:

> The eensy, weensy spider
> Climbed up the water spout.
> Down came the rain
> And washed the spider out.
> Out came the sun
> And dried up all the rain.
> And the eensy, weensey spider
> Went up the spout again.

Popcorn

While popping corn with the children, tell them how popcorn was discovered. Say, "American Indians invented popcorn. They would put a big flat rock on their campfire and let it heat up. When the rock was hot, they would throw kernels of corn onto it. The moisture inside the corn kernels got hot and popped the kernels open."

Remember to read *Popcorn* to the children. (See "October Storytime.")

Nut Hunt

Hide real or paper acorns around the classroom. Give the children 3–5 minutes to hunt for the acorns, then have each child count what he or she found. Sitting in a circle, have the children take turns telling how many acorns they have.

Write each child's acorn number on a piece of paper. Instruct the children to glue the number in the middle of a sheet of construction paper and glue their paper or real acorns around the number. (You can play this game with any seasonal shape.)

Cat and Mouse Game

Have the children sit in a circle and choose one child to be the CAT. That child should then leave the room and 3–4 other children should be given small cards bearing a picture of a MOUSE.

Each MOUSE should sit on their card to hide it from the CAT. When the CAT returns, all the children must hide their faces. Each MOUSE makes squeaking noises, and the CAT tries to identify each MOUSE by listening for the direction from which the sound comes. When the CAT picks a child suspected of being a MOUSE, that child stands up. When all the MICE have been found, a new CAT and new MICE are chosen and the game continues. (If you have a small group of children, use one MOUSE.)

———————————— LETTER RECOGNITION ————————————

Sandpaper A

Make sandpaper A for tactile reinforcement of the shape of A. With a pencil, make a large A on a sheet of construction paper for each child. Go over it with glue, then have each sprinkle sand on their A. Shake off any excess sand. Let it dry. Have the children "feel" the A.

Craft Stick A

Have your children paint three craft sticks with tempera paint. When dry, glue them together to form an A.

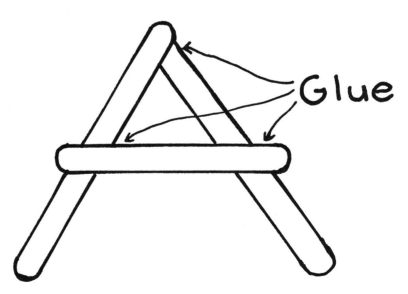

Rectangle A

With your paper cutter, cut a pile of 3″ × ½″ rectangles. Give each child three rectangles and a piece of construction paper. Ask them to make an A with the rectangles on the paper. When they do so, you can glue it in place. Then instruct them to count out three more rectangles from your pile to make another A. Repeat the procedure until the construction paper is covered with As.

The As Are Hiding

Make a copy of "The As Are Hiding" worksheet for each child. Say, "Can you find the As that are hiding in this picture? With your black marker or crayon, go over each A you find. Then color the picture."

—————————— MUSIC AND MOVEMENT ——————————

I'm a Little Acorn

Sing this to the tune of "I'm a Little Teapot":

> I'm a little acorn
> Short and stout. (*bow arms out*)
> Plant me in the ground (*squat down*)
> And I'll grow a sprout. (*stick one arm up in the air*)

The Tightrope Walker

Set up a balance beam and "course" for the children to walk around the room. For example: "Go up the slide, down the slide, walk over to the balance beam, go across the balance beam, around the table in the housekeeping corner, touch the easel, then get back to the end of the line." The children will all follow each other.

While doing this, play a circus record or the song "The Tightrope Walker" on the album *Pre-K Fitness,* available from Melody House.

All Fall Down

Find a nice fall tree outside and have your children join hands in a circle around it. Sing this song to the tune of "Ring Around the Rosey" while walking around the tree:

> Ring around the trees,
> Pocket full of leaves.
> Autumn, Autumn,
> All fall down. (*drop hands and fall down*)

Acorn Roll

After the children "all fall down" (from the previous song), have them stay in place and pretend to be acorns. Sing:

I'm a little acorn sitting on the ground
When the fall wind blows I roll 'round and 'round. (*in a sitting position, children grasp knees and roll away from the tree*)

SONGS, POEMS, AND FINGERPLAYS

One, Two, Buckle My Shoe

Do actions for each phrase:

> One, two,
> Buckle my shoe.
> Three, four,
> Shut the door.
> Five, six,
> Pick up sticks.
> Seven, eight,
> Lay them straight.
> Nine, ten,
> A big fat hen!

Fall

> The leaves are green, the nuts are brown.
> They hang so high, they will never come down.
> Leave them alone till the bright fall weather,
> And then they will all come down together.

Two Little Blackbirds

> Two little blackbirds sitting on a hill (*index fingers behind back*)
> One named Jack (*bring out one finger*)
> One named Jill (*bring out other finger*)
> Fly away Jack (*put one finger behind back*)
> Fly away Jill (*put other finger behind back*)
> Come back, Jack (*bring out one finger*)
> Come back, Jill. (*bring out other finger*)

FROM BUTTON'S COUNTRY KITCHEN

Orange Brew

Put the following ingredients into a blender and whip:

2 6–ounce cans frozen orange juice	2 teaspoons vanilla
1 cup water	20 ice cubes
2 cups milk	

Pour into individual cups and eat with a spoon.

Orange Gelatin

2 family-size packages OR 4 small packages orange gelatin
2½ cups boiling water

Completely dissolve the gelatin in boiling water. Pour into a 13″ × 9″ pan. Chill until firm, about 3 hours. To unmold: Dip the pan in warm water for about 15 seconds. Then cut the gelatin into squares or use a pumpkin cookie cutter. Lift the pieces from the pan and enjoy.

Brownies

4 ounces unsweetened chocolate	3 eggs
⅔ cup shortening	1¼ cups flour
1 cup sugar	1 teaspoon baking powder
½ cup brown sugar	1 teaspoon salt

Preheat the oven to 350°F. Lightly grease a 13″ × 19″ × 2″ pan. Melt the chocolate and shortening in a saucepan over low heat. Remove from the heat and mix in the remaining ingredients. Spread the batter in the pan and bake for 30 minutes. When cool, cut into squares.

Toasted Pumpkin Seeds

Cut open a pumpkin and scoop out the seeds. Wash and dry the seeds and put them in a plastic bag. Add a small amount of oil and salt. Shake to mix. Then place the seeds in a shallow baking dish or cookie sheet. Bake at 350°F for 20–25 minutes until brown. Let the seeds cool. Then crack them open and enjoy.

You might want to save some unbaked seeds and plant them in the spring.

───────────── VIDEOS FOR OCTOBER ─────────────

The Ugly Duckling (Troll © 1990, Mahwah, NJ)

Cher narrates this classic tale of the lonely, rejected ugly duckling who finally discovers he's a swan. This is a good video to begin a discussion about feelings.

───────────── WORKSHEETS FOR OCTOBER ─────────────

The following worksheets are referred to in this month's readiness activities.

Let's Build a Haunted House

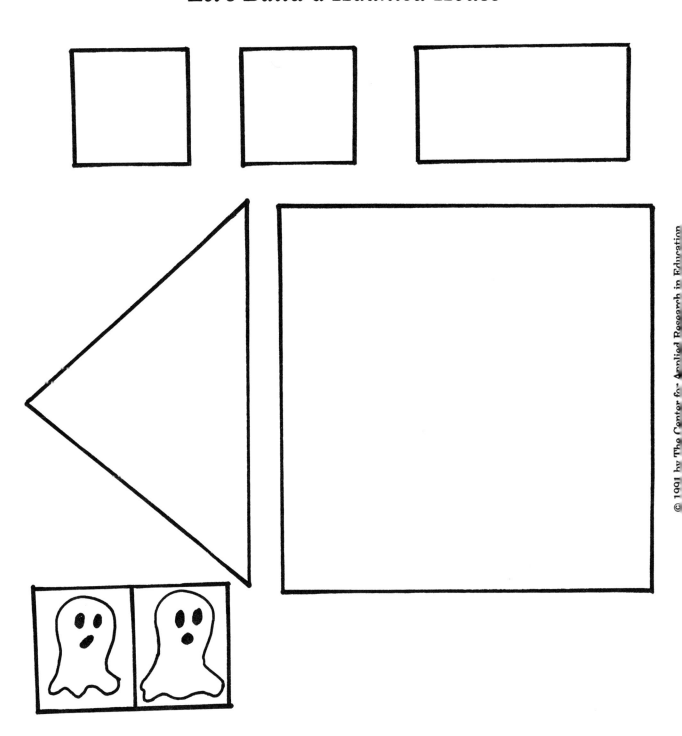

Follow-the-Numbers Pumpkin

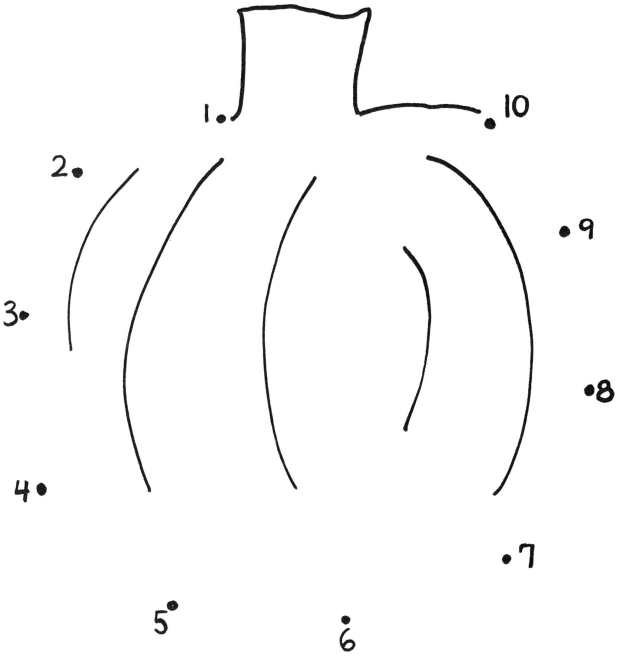

69

Gus Ghost   Goody Ghost

Great Ghost   Go Ghost

How Many Jack-o'Lanterns on the Fence?

Carrots

Pumpkin and Jack-o'-Lantern Mask

Build a Witch

Smiley and Sad

Spiders, Spiders

An Acorn Person

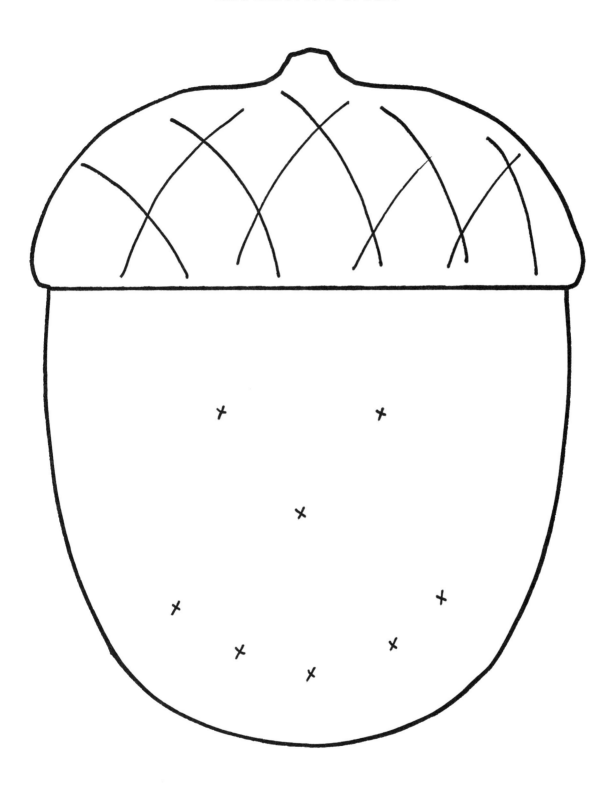

Watch the Acorn

Nuts and More Nuts!

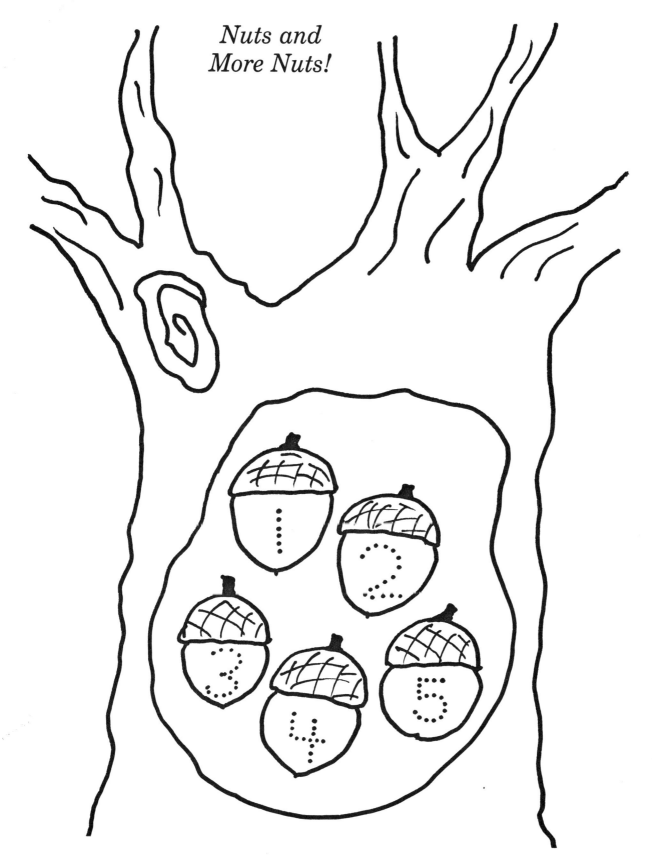

A Football Mum

Sizes of Pumpkins

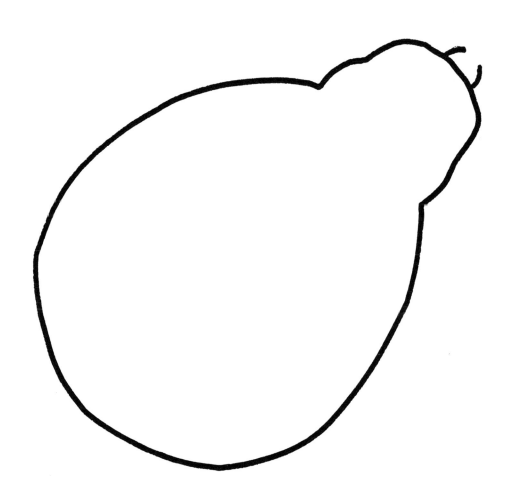

The As Are Hiding

November—
A Harvest of Fun

A cornucopia of activities centered around harvest
time greets the children this month. Food, nutrition,
Pilgrims, and Indians abound!

Beginnings

Dear Parents:

During this month we will be concentrating on food, nutrition, and the Pilgrims and Indians. The children will be involved in learning about healthy foods and will have fun doing projects that increase their awareness of good food.

We will be discussing the "First Thanksgiving" and the many ways the Indians helped the Pilgrims survive in America.

We will conclude this Thanksgiving unit by celebrating with our own version of a Thanksgiving feast here in class. I will be asking each child to bring one "ingredient" for our feast—a flyer will follow.

My "thanks" for sharing your child with me!

Sincerely,

_____

© 1991 by The Center for Applied Research in Education

The following stories introduce your students to the meaning of Thanksgiving, as well as to the wonderful things they can see in the world.

Arthur's Thanksgiving by MARC BROWN (Little, Brown & Co.)

This delightfully illustrated book finds Arthur in a predicament. Arthur, the director of his school's Thanksgiving play, can't find anyone to play the part of the turkey. After much ado, Arthur decides he'll have to play the part himself. When the day of the play arrives, Arthur's classmates decide to help him out. Arthur winds up with a whole stage full of turkeys and a lot of new friends.

You might want your class to put on a turkey skit with everyone playing a turkey. See November's "Songs, Poems, and Fingerplays."

Don't Eat Too Much Turkey by LILLIAN HOBAN (Greenwillow Books)

A first-grade class celebrates Thanksgiving. The caring and sharing that should be an inherent part of the celebration comes slowly but surely to the children. This is a nice book to read before your class Thanksgiving celebration.

Ingrid Our Turtle by PETER LIPPMAN (Golden Press)

Ingrid lives in a garden in Selden-by-the-Sea. Because it takes so long for Ingrid to get anywhere, she never has gotten to see the world. Taking a clue from a passing train, Ingrid decides she can "chug" her way around the world—and she does!

This Old Man—The Country Song by ROBIN MICHAEL KOONTZ (Dodd, Mead & Company)

This is a colorful, upbeat book to get children to sing and count to the tune of "This Old Man." It provides good reinforcement of numeral recognition and rhyming. Ten little old men, in numbered sweatshirts, take you through the numbers from one to ten in comical antics on an otherwise peaceful farm.

Sometimes It's Turkey, Sometimes It's Feathers by LORNA BALIAN (Abingdon Press)

Mrs. Gumm hatches a turkey from a speckled egg she found. She and her cat proceed to fatten up the young bird for the upcoming Thanksgiving feast. However, when Thanksgiving arrives, the plump turkey shares in the feast as a friend loved by Mrs. Gumm.

This is a good book to begin a Thanksgiving discussion about families, especially nontraditional families.

You might also have the children make the finger puppet described in the "Wattles the Turkey" activity.

Colors by JOHN J. REISS (Bradbury Press)

A burst of vivid color brings the delight of observing the wonderful world around us to your classroom. This is a good book for color recognition and the naming of common objects.

Have your preschoolers find all the things in the classroom that are as red as an apple and so on.

———— READINESS ACTIVITIES FOR NOVEMBER ————

Tilly Turtle

In anticipation of winter, turtles eat all they can during the fall. Most turtles eat only vegetables. Sometimes they eat too much and can't fit back into their shells when they want to sleep. If this happens, they stop eating for a few days and try again. In October, most land turtles dig holes in the ground. They hibernate in their holes until spring. The length of sleep depends on the climate.

Look for pictures of turtles in books and children's encyclopedias. Review the many sizes and colors of turtles from the massive leather backs to the beautiful painted turtles.

Make a copy of the "Tilly Turtle" worksheet for each child. Have the children color the shell like one of the turtles pictured in the books. Have them add four legs, head, and neck.

Feeling "Raisiny"

Bring in some grapes and raisins for the children to feel, smell, and eat. Explain that raisins are dried grapes. Small, sweet, seedless grapes are the best to use to make raisins. Raisins contain large quantities of natural sugar, iron, and vitamins.

Make a copy of the "Feeling 'Raisiny'" worksheet for each child. Explain that the faces show ways we all feel at some time or another. Discuss each feeling. Start by telling the children about a time when you were surprised, angry, sad, or happy. Let the children discuss their own experiences and feelings—but don't force any child if he or she doesn't want to. After each feelings discussion, have the children color in the raisins on the worksheet.

Have a supply of raisins on hand for the children to enjoy after completing the worksheet. Or, let the children place real raisins on the worksheet and eat them when the activity is completed.

Wattles the Turkey

One of the first large birds to be seen by the Pilgrims was the turkey. The turkey is found only in North and Central America. On a turkey's head is a wattle, which consists of folds of thin skin. When a turkey becomes angry, the wattle fills up with blood and turns a bright red color.

Make a copy of the "Wattles the Turkey" worksheet for each child. Say, "Color Wattles' eyes, beak and wattle. Color his head, neck, and body brown. Color each feather a different color. Then cut out all your pieces." You should cut out the two finger holes for the children. Then have them glue the feathers onto the back of Wattles' body.

When completed and dried, have the children insert their index and middle fingers in the holes—these are Wattles' legs, so that he can waddle around. (If you make Wattles' body out of oaktag, the finger puppet will last much longer.)

Be sure to read *Sometimes It's Turkey, Sometimes It's Feathers* (see "November Storytime").

Community Helper—The Police Officer

Introduce this activity by saying, "Police officers protect us and help us. They tell us never to talk to strangers when we're not with an adult, and never to take candy from someone we don't know. They remind us never to run into the street. Police officers know all about safety. If you are ever lost and see a police officer, tell the officer your name and the officer will help you find the person you were with. The people in the police department help keep our neighborhoods safe."

Make a copy of "The Police Officer" worksheet for each child. Have the children color the mask and cut it out. Have them give the officer hair, a nose, and a mouth. You should cut out the eye holes for the children, and then have the children glue a craft stick onto the back of the mask for a handle. Ask the children to put on their mask and remember one safety tip that their police officer would say to the class. Your children can take turns being "the officer" and act out some of the many ways police officers help us.

If any of the children's parents are police officers, invite them to class. You can also call your local police precinct and ask if there is an officer who visits classrooms, or ask if you can visit the precinct.

My School and Me

Make a copy of the "My School and Me" worksheet for each child. Then say, "Here is a picture of your new school and you. Color your school. Make each part of your school—roof, doors, windows—a different color. Now color yourself."

Cut out the rectangle of the child on each preschooler's worksheet. Cut on the two solid lines around the door. Fold the door back on the dotted line. Put glue around the edge of the child's picutre (excluding the bottom edge). From the back of the school, glue the child in the doorway.

"Sour Grapes"

You will need a copy of the "Grapes" worksheet for each child, small paper cups, coffee stirrers, small pieces of sponge, and red and blue tempera paints.

Grapes are an easy-to-eat, healthful, natural snack that come in many varieties.

The old fable about the fox who couldn't reach the succulent grapes and then decided he "didn't want them anyway because for sure they are sour" is a good story to tell your children. (It's even better if you act it out!) The children readily come to their own conclusions about the fox's reasoning. Discuss ways the fox could have gotten the grapes.

To spark interest in the science of color mixing, say, "I want to make a bunch of grapes for that silly fox but I don't have any purple paint. (*Hold up jar of red paint.*) I'll help. (*Hold up jar of blue paint.*) I'll help, too!"

Then spoon into each child's cup a spoonful of each color. Let the children mix the two colors. Show the children how to dip the end of a small piece of sponge into the paint. Place the sponge in the center of a grape on the worksheet and turn it around in a circle. Pick it up and repeat on the other grapes.

An Apple Puzzle

Make a copy of "An Apple Puzzle" worksheet for each child. Then have the children color all the apple halves and cut out all the squares. Ask them to match the numbers on the apple halves with the correct number of seeds.

Fishing for Your Dinner

Make a copy of the "Thanksgiving Dinner" worksheet for each child. Have the children color the food items and then cut out all the pieces. Tape a paper clip onto each piece and place the pieces on a paper plate on the floor. Then tie a small magnet onto a piece of 3-foot-long string. While holding onto the end of the string, the children will stand over the dinner to see what they can catch.

When done, have the children glue the dinner items on the corners of a piece of construction paper to use as a Thanksgiving placemat.

Indian Corn

Corn was the main source of food for many American Indian tribes. The Indians taught the Pilgrims how to plant and grow corn. For fertilizer, the Indians would put a dead fish in each hole with the corn seed.

Show the children real Indian corn and let them feel the hard, smooth kernels. You might also show them pictures of this beautiful variety of corn.

Make a copy of the "Indian Corn" worksheet for each child. Have the children color the kernels this way: 1—RED, 2—YELLOW, 3—ORANGE.

Vegetables—Above and Below

Bring in some vegetables that grow above the ground, and that grow below the ground. Let the children feel, smell, and classify each.

Make a copy of the "Vegetables—Above and Below" worksheet for each child. Have the children put their finger on a vegetable that grows below the ground. Have them color that vegetable. Now have them find the other below-ground vegetable and color that one. Ask, "Which of these four vegetables have you had lately? Make sure you try new vegetables when they are served at home or when you eat out."

All the Colors of the Rainbow

Arrange prisms on a table in the sun. Allow the children to move and turn the prisms so that they can visually experience the beautiful colors of the rainbow.

Fun with Peanuts

Make these projects with your children. They can paint the peanuts first, then add details with a marker, paper, or "natural" ingredients.

Peanut Fish

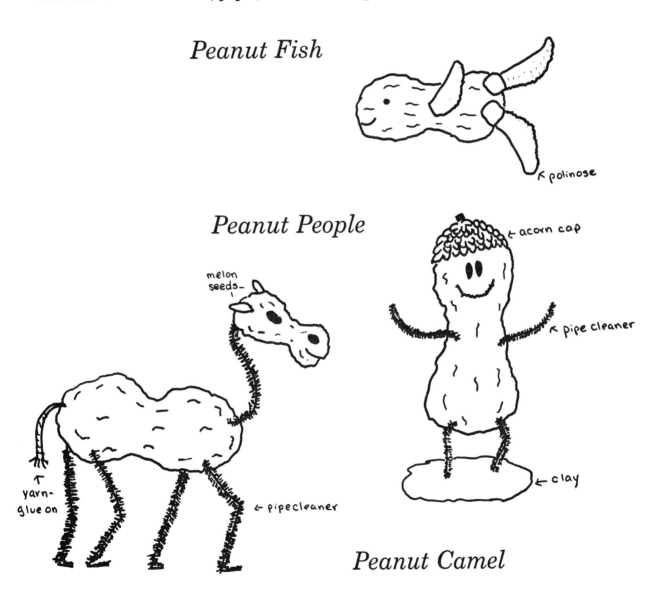

Peanut People

Peanut Camel

Yummy Peanuts

Although peanuts are called nuts, they are really not nuts at all. They are pod fruit like beans. Peanuts grow underground and are very high in protein. Hundreds of products have been made from the peanut and its vines. Peanut butter is probably the most delicious one! Have the children shell some peanuts and make peanut butter in a blender. Just grind the peanuts (and add a little oil for smoothness). Use the peanut butter as a dip with carrot sticks or celery sticks, or make "ants on a log" (celery sticks stuffed with peanut butter and dotted with raisins).

Make a copy of the "Yummy Peanuts" worksheet for each child. Then say, "Color these big peanuts light brown. Give each of them eyes, nose, mouth, arms, and legs."

The Peanut Scientist

Dr. George Washington Carver discovered hundreds of uses for the peanut. In his laboratory, he made soap, coffee, ink, cheese, flour, and many more products from peanuts.

Rainbow Trout Fish Kite

Fish was a popular and nutritious food of the Pilgrims and Indians. Fish is a very healthful food that contains protein, vitamins, and minerals.

Make a copy of the "Rainbow Trout" worksheet for each child. Say, "Color the fish in rainbow colors. Then cut out the fish. Punch a hole at the top (by the mouth) and tie a piece of string about three feet long. Hold the end of your string and run with your fish (in a safe place). Watch your fish fly!" You may want to put a piece of tape on the fish before punching the hole so that the paper will have some rip resistance.

My Thanksgiving Book

Make a copy of "My Thanksgiving Book" (two worksheet pages) for each child. Have them cut the eight boxes apart and staple them in the top left-hand corner. Tell your children the Thanksgiving story as they turn the pages of their Thanksgiving book. Then let the children color a page or two each day. Be sure to rediscuss the story each day. When they've finished the book, the children can take their books home and tell the story to their families.

Friends

The Pilgrims invited the Indians to a great feast—the first Thanksgiving—to thank them for teaching the colonists how to hunt, fish, and plant their crops.

Make a copy of the "Friends" worksheet for each child. Say, "Color these two friends. Go over the letters of the word FRIENDS."

Breakfast, Lunch, and Dinner

Collect a supply of supermarket circulars, and give one to each child. Have the children then cut out food and/or package pictures. Make a poster on the bulletin board with three paper plates entitled: BREAKFAST, LUNCH, DINNER. Glue the foods onto the appropriate plate.

Fill the Cornucopia

Make copies of the cornucopia and fruits/vegetables worksheet. Have the children sit in a circle with the cornucopia in the middle. Give each child a picture of a fall fruit or vegetable, a real item, or a plastic item. (If more than eight children are playing, have two children be each fruit or vegetable.) Sing the following to the tune of "Where Is Thumbkin?"

CLASS:	Where is corn? Where is corn?
CHILD WITH CORN:	Here I am. Here I am. (*holds up corn*)
CLASS:	How are you this morning?
CHILD WITH CORN:	Very well, I thank you.
CLASS:	Run away. Run away. (*child with corn gets up and runs around the circle once or twice and then puts the corn on the cornucopia*)
CLASS:	Where is apple? Where is apple?
CHILD WITH APPLE:	Here I am. Here I am. (*holds up apple*)
CLASS:	How are you this morning?
CHILD WITH APPLE:	Very well, I thank you.
CLASS:	Run away. Run away. (*child with apple gets up and runs around the circle once or twice and then puts the apple on the cornucopia*)

The game continues in the same way with the other fruits and vegetables.

MUSIC AND MOVEMENT

Autumn's Here

The leaves come softly down. (*wiggle fingers while moving hands downward*)
They settle softly on the ground. (*stop wiggling fingers*)
Then, SWISH, the wind comes whirling by (*move fingers up in the air and twirl around*)
And sends them dancing in the sky. (*wiggle fingers all around*)

Row, Row, Row Your Canoe

Have the children sit cross-legged on the floor in pairs, with one child behind the other. Make enough copies of the paddles worksheet so that each child has one paddle. The children should paddle while they sing:

> Row, row, row your canoe
> Gently down the stream.
> Merrily, merrily, merrily, merrily,
> Life is but a dream.

Ask the children to switch their paddles to the other side and sing again.

—————— SONGS, POEMS, AND FINGERPLAYS ——————

Turkey's Song

> "Gobble, gobble," says the turkey;
> Soon will be Thanksgiving Day.
> I can't believe what you say!
> So you say you'll eat me;
> That's no way to treat me.
> Then I will run away!

Way Up in an Apple Tree

> Way up in an apple tree (*hold fists in the air*)
> Two little apples smiled at me.
> I shook the tree as hard as I could. (*make shaking motion with hands*)
> Down came the apples—
> And mmmm! were they good! (*rub tummy*)

Ten Little Indians

Sit with the children in a circle and sing the following song. When you point to a child, that child should stand up. Be sure to repeat the song enough times to include all the children.

> One little, two little, three little Indians,
> Four little, five little, six little Indians,
> Seven little, eight little, nine little Indians,
> Ten little Indian children.

Turkeys One and All

Make turkey feather collars for each child: (1) Cut out colorful paper feathers, (2) staple or tape these onto a piece of yarn, (3) loosely tie the yarn around the child's neck. When all the children have their turkey feather collars, recite and act out "Little Turkeys":

We're all little turkeys in a row. (*children hold hands*)
Wind us up and watch us go. (*children turn backs to each other and "wind up" each other*)
We waddle, waddle, waddle, waddle, waddle we. (*waddle*)
We waddle, waddle, waddle, waddle, waddle we. (*continue waddling around the room*)

—————— FROM BUTTON'S COUNTRY KITCHEN ——————

Baking Powder Biscuits

2 cups flour   2 tablespoons butter
4 teaspoons baking powder   ¾ cup milk
1 teaspoon salt

Preheat the oven to 450°F. Stir the flour, baking powder, and salt in a mixing bowl. Cut up the butter and add it to the flour mixture. Add the milk a little at a time. Knead the dough with well-floured hands. Roll the dough out on a floured surface to about ½" thickness. Cut out biscuits with a cutter and place on an ungreased cookie sheet. Bake 12–15 minutes or until golden.

Apple Crisp

3 cups sliced apples   2 teaspoons lemon juice
½ cup packed brown sugar   1 teaspoon cinnamon
¼ cup soft butter   ½ cup flour

Preheat the oven to 375°F. Spread the apples in a baking pan. Sprinkle with lemon juice. Combine the brown sugar, flour, soft butter, and cinnamon. Crumble this mixture over the apples and bake for 25 minutes.

Cinnamon Toast

Mix together 3 tablespoons sugar and 1 tablespoon cinnamon. Sprinkle this over buttered toast. Place the toast in a warm oven to slightly melt the sugar.

Baked Apples

Wash and core an apple for each child. Place the apples in a shallow baking dish. In each apple, put 1 tablespoon sugar and a dash of cinnamon and nutmeg. Add enough water to cover the bottom of the dish. Bake at 400°F for about 30 minutes or until apples are soft. Baste apples with their own juice.

Corn Bread

1¼ cups flour	¼ cup sugar
¾ cup corn meal	1 well-beaten egg
3 teaspoons baking powder	¾ cup milk
1 teaspoon salt	¼ cup melted margarine

Mix together the flour, corn meal, baking powder, salt, and sugar. Combine and add the egg, milk, and margarine. Stir until just moistened. Pour into a greased, shallow pan. Bake in a 400°F oven for 20 minutes.

VIDEOS FOR NOVEMBER

The Little Red Hen (Golden Book Video, Western Publishing Co., Racine, WI 1985)

The Dog, the Cat, and the Rat invent excuses to avoid helping the Little Red Hen. They learn the lesson of this old tale: those who do not work will not eat! Also included in this 30–minute video are "The Tale of Peter Rabbit" and "Polly's Pet." This is a good tape to go along with a cooking project.

WORKSHEETS FOR NOVEMBER

The following worksheets are referred to in this month's readiness activities.

Tilly Turtle

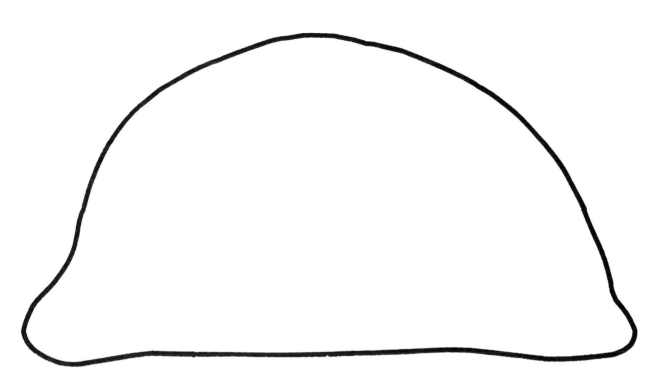

Feeling "Raisiny"

Happy

Sad

Angry

Surprised

Wattles the Turkey

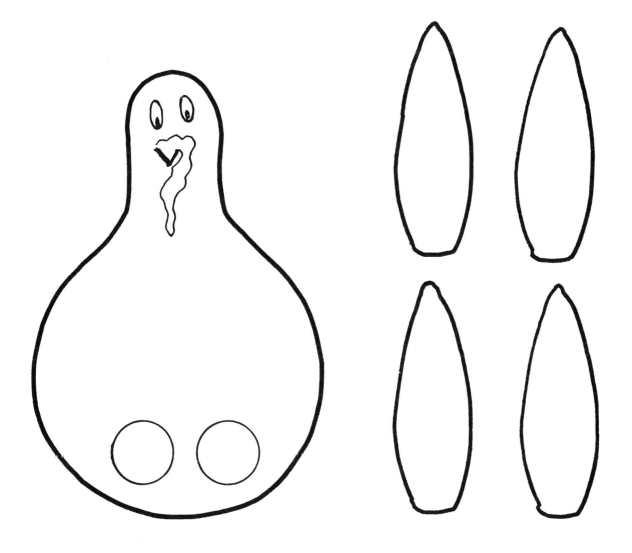

The Police Officer

100

My School and Me

PRESCHOOL

Grapes

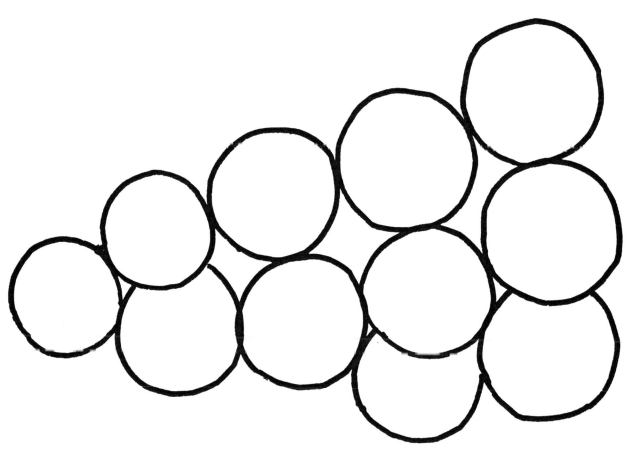

An Apple Puzzle

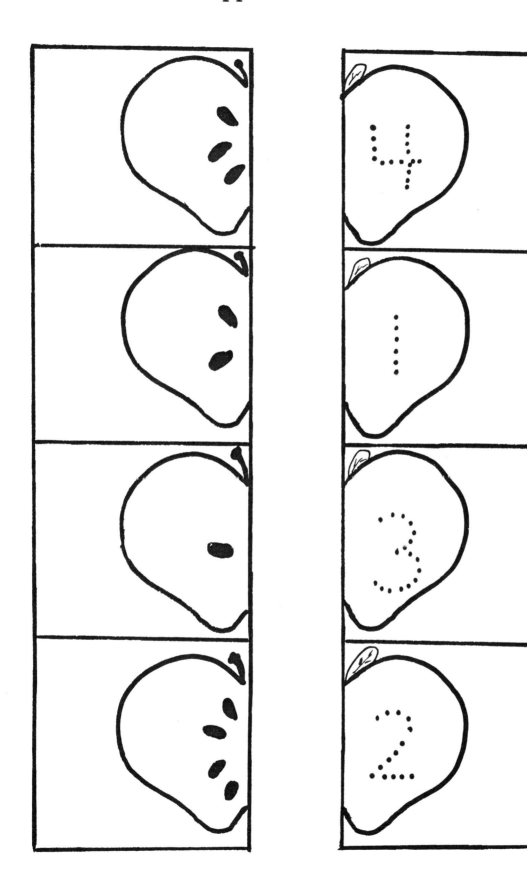

Thanksgiving Dinner

Indian Corn

Vegetables—Above and Below

potatoes

cucumbers

peppers

Carrots

Yummy Peanuts

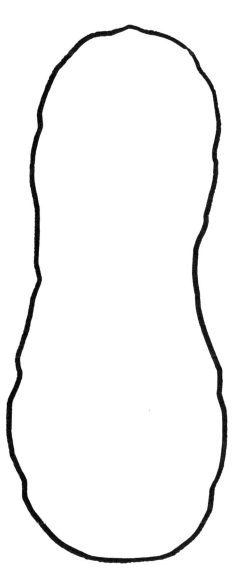
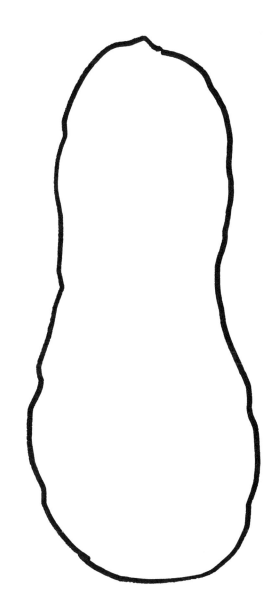

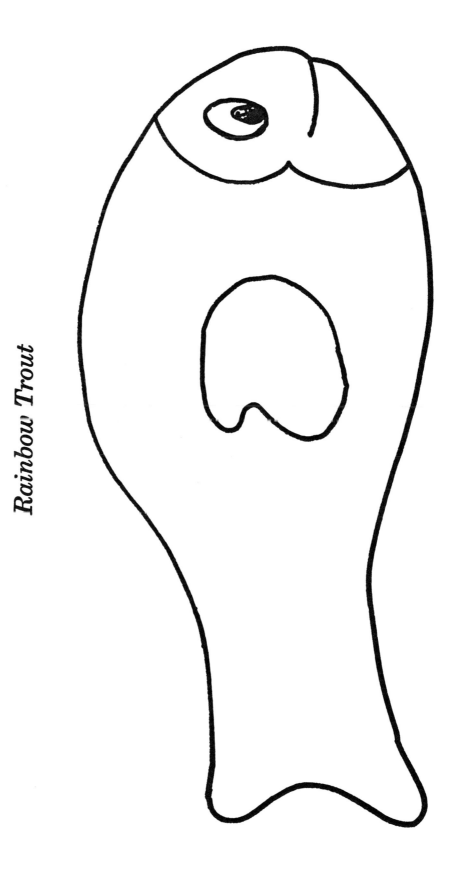

Rainbow Trout

4.

5.

6.

7.

110

Friends

Cornucopia

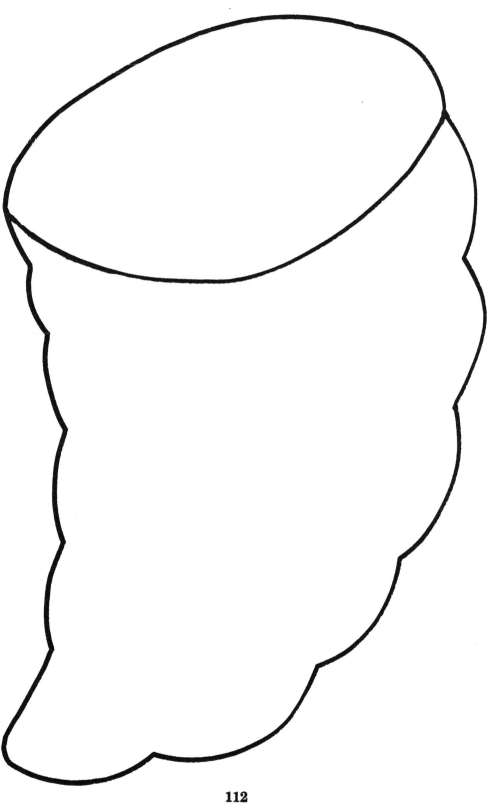

112

Paddles

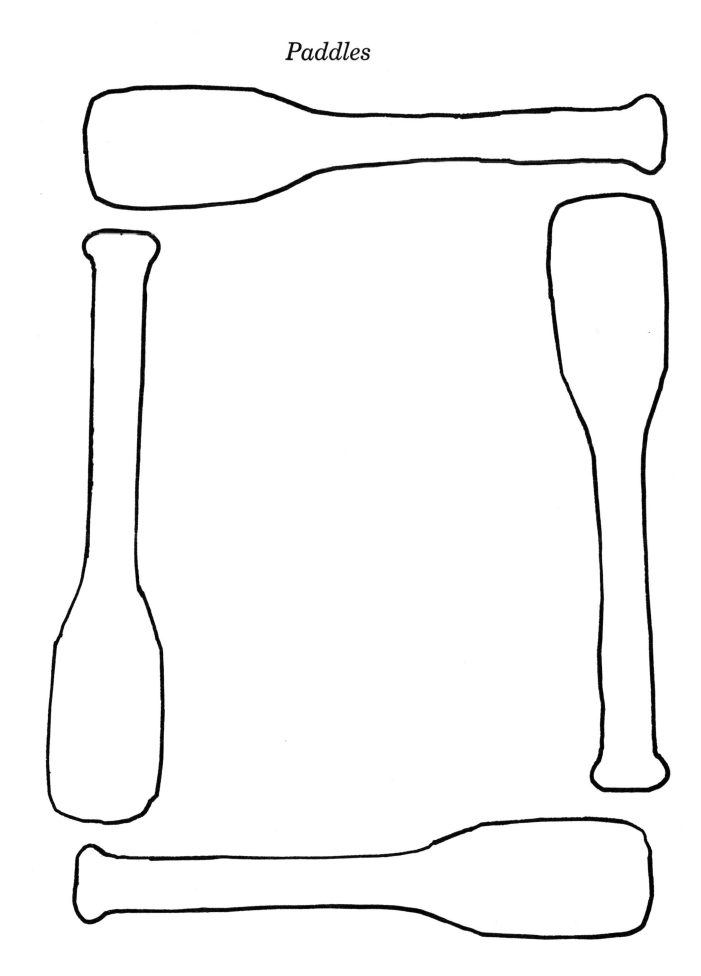

Enchanting December

December has arrived with its exciting holidays and wintry weather. The projects in this section are designed to enhance your children's cognitive development regarding the season of winter, as well as add to the glow of their holiday happenings!

Beginnings

DECEMBER

Dear Parents:

This winter month of December is filled with exciting things for the children to learn about and enjoy. The festivities of the holdiays bring joy and warmth that envelop both your child's home and school lives.

"Hibernation" and "migration" are two words your child will be learning about. Involving the children in the world of nature and its effects on animals will make them begin to realize the wonderful world that exists outside of their homes.

We look forward to sharing the joys and wonders of this holiday season together.

Sincerely,

_____

The following stories let your students experience the sights and sounds of the season.

The Christmas Gift by EMILY ARNOLD McCULLY (Harper & Row)

This beautiful and wordless book of watercolor pictures tells about the excitement of the Christmas season—the sights, the sounds, the smells, and the love. These pictures are worth a thousand words!

After telling the story to your class as a group, it's nice to sit with each child individually and ask the child to tell you what's happening on each page.

The Berenstain Bears Meet Santa Bear by STAN AND JAN BERENSTAIN (Random House)

The sights and sounds of Christmas are all over Bear Country, and the bear family gets caught up in the frenzy. A delightful ending shows the cubs experiencing the real joys of Christmas.

After reading the book, discuss the joys of being nice to friends and family with the children. Make the "I Care and Share" medallion. Photocopy as many medallions as you need, glue them onto either cardboard or oaktag, and cut them out. With markers, have each child draw their face in the circle. Punch a hole in the top of the medallion and string it with yarn. Present each child with their medallion and a big "I'm proud of *you.*"

The Fox With Cold Feet by BILL SINGER (Parents Magazine Press)

It's winter in the forest and the first snow has covered the ground. The self-proclaimed "quick and spry, clever and sly" fox has cold feet. He unsuccessfully tries to outsmart his forest friends in this silly, entertaining tale.

Do the "Guess Who Belongs to This Foot!" and "Footprint Number Practice" activities in December's readiness section.

Sylvester Bear Overslept by JANE WAHL (Parents Magazine Press)

Sylvester and Phyllis Bear prepare for their coming winter nap by preparing and eating 35 apple pies! Phyllis' snoring sends Sylvester to seek a new hibernating place. The bears sadly lose each other, but are soon happily reunited—with Sylvester deciding that Phyllis' snoring isn't so bad after all.

The project "P.J. the Christmas Bear" is a good follow-up to this story.

Bini's First Chanukah by JANE BRESKIN ZALBEN (Henry Holt and Co.)

This simple, poignant story tells of Bini Bear's and his family's preparation for Chanukah. The pastel illustrations capture all the warmth and joy of this timeless celebration. The story includes Mama's holiday latkes recipe!

The dreidel chain activity in December's readiness section fits in well after this story.

Santa's Moose by SYD HOFF (Harper & Row)

Milton the moose wants to help Santa Claus on Christmas Eve. He gets discouraged though by his own clumsiness. Santa and his reindeer remind Milton that "all it takes is practice." Santa's moose perseveres and gets the job done.

Make your own Santa's moose using the pattern given in this month's readiness section.

Little Christmas Elf by EILEEN CURRAN (Troll Associates)

Little Simon the elf tries hard, but accomplishes little in Santa's workshop. Santa himself decides to help Simon. Through mutual cooperation, the job gets done.

Snow Lion by DAVID McPHAIL (Parents Magazine Press)

The heat of the jungle makes Mr. Lion venture into the mountains, where he discovers snow. After he unsuccessfully tries to bring some back to his friends in the jungle, he decides to bring his friends to the snow instead. All the animals have a delightful time and make a snow lion as a "thank you" to the lion who showed them a "cool" way to have fun.

Bring in some snow in a pan or bowl and let the children observe it melting. If no snow is available, use ice cubes.

READINESS ACTIVITIES FOR DECEMBER

The Triangle Tree

Make a copy of the "Triangle Tree" worksheet for each child. Say, "1. Color the triangles at the bottom of this page. Use bright holiday colors. Put some dots on them. 2. Color the trunk brown. 3. Cut out the colored triangles and glue them onto the tree. 4. You can add glue and glitter, pieces of ribbon, or colored tissue to your tree."

P.J. the Christmas Bear

Make a copy of the "P.J. the Christmas Bear" worksheet for each child. Say, "It's Christmas Eve and P.J. is ready for bed. Color P.J. brown. Color his pajamas, cap, and slippers in red and green stripes. Then cut out P.J. and his clothes. Glue P.J.'s pajamas onto him. Glue the cap onto his head, and his slippers onto his feet. Goodnight, P.J. Sweet dreams!"

Be sure to read *Sylvester Bear Overslept* (from December's storytime section).

A Dreidel Chain

Chanukah (or Hanukkah) is often called the Festival of Lights because candles are lit in Jewish homes and synagogues. During this eight-day celebration, children play games with a dreidel.

Make a dreidel chain using the "Dreidel Chain" worksheet. Make a copy of the worksheet for each child, and have the children color the dreidels and cut them out. Help them to punch holes where shown. Then string and knot the dreidels on a length of yarn that is long enough to hang around the children's necks.

Be sure to read *Bini's First Chanukah* (see "December Storytime").

Rudolph Mobile

Make a copy of the "Rudolph Mobile" worksheet for each child. Say, "Rudolph is taking Santa Claus on a test ride around the world. Color the land on the earth green and the water blue. Color Rudolph's nose red and his body brown. Color Santa and his sleigh." Then cut out everything and string them as shown to make a mobile.

Shhh!

The animals of the forest and the fish in the pond have gone to sleep for the winter. They are hibernating. Animals hibernate because food is scarce in the winter and it's too cold to be walking around. The tops of ponds and streams freeze as well as the earth. Many animals dig holes deep in the ground and curl up for a long winter sleep. Frogs bury themselves in mud at the bottoms of ponds. Snakes crawl into cracks in rocks, and fish go to the bottoms of the deepest parts of ponds. Bears sleep for most of the winter in caves.

Take a look at some fish in a fish tank. Ask, "Why don't they have to hibernate?"

Hibernating Worms

Make a copy of the "Hibernating Worms" worksheet for each child. Help the children with the directions if necessary.

After completing the worksheet, have the children make some clay worms.

Hibernating Fish

Make a copy of the "Hibernating Fish" worksheet for each child. Say, "The water is too cold at the top of the pond, so this fish family wants to hibernate at the bottom of the pond. Color the pond blue. Then color, cut out, and glue the fish family in the pond. How many fish are there?"

Reddy the Robin

One of North America's most well-known birds, the robin red breast, flies to the Gulf Coast for the winter.

Make a copy of the "Reddy the Robin" worksheet for each child. (The patterns can be traced onto construction paper to make the project sturdier.)

Say, "Color Reddy's breast red, his head black, and his body and wings brown. Cut Reddy out. Cut the slit on his body for the wings, and insert the wings. Then color and cut out his suitcase. Put the suitcase on Reddy's wing. Reddy is now ready to go!"

Guess Who Belongs to This Foot!

Trace one of each child's feet onto a piece of construction paper. Then have each child trace and cut out their foot. Lay each cut-out foot on another piece of construction paper. Go around the foot to make a sock, and add a cuff. Have the children decorate the sock with stripes and dots. Cut out the sock and staple as shown. Write the name of each child on the back of the sock.

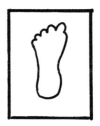

You can make a bulletin board display of the socks or decorate your classroom door. Be sure, too, to read *The Fox With Cold Feet* (see "December Storytime").

Footprint Number Practice

Make a set of number footprints as shown. Use oaktag or construction paper covered with clear self-stick vinyl, or use actual shoe insoles and a black permanent marker.

Mix up the footprints. Then have each child put them in order and "walk" on them, saying the numbers as they move from one number to another.

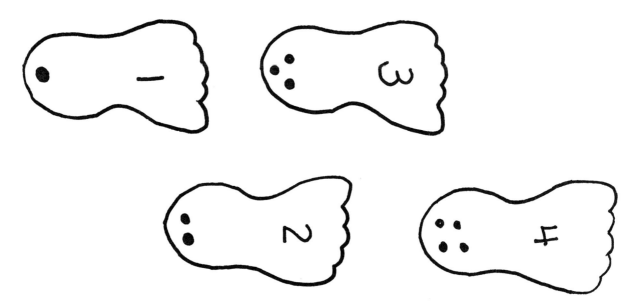

Pine Cone Feeder

Explain to the children that many birds do *not* fly to warmer temperatures in the winter. For these birds, food should be placed outdoors so that they do not go hungry.

Give each child a small paper cup of peanut butter. Show them how to scoop up some peanut butter with the tip of their finger and wipe it onto the edges of a pine cone. Continue around the pine cone. Then sprinkle on bird seed. Tie a string at the top of the pine cone and hang it from a tree branch.

Freckles the Fish

Make a copy of the "Freckles the Fish" worksheet for each child. Say, "It's winter and the top of Freckle's pond is frozen. But she's safe and warm near the mud at the bottom of the pond. Use your crayons to color Freckles. Then use your brown and black crayons to color in some mud at the bottom of the pond. Now make a wash of a half cup of water and a half spoonful of blue tempera paint. Brush the wash over your entire piece of paper. Freckles' crayoned body will resist the wash. After your picture has dried, use a piece of white chalk to add some ice to the top of the pond."

A Freckles Mobile

Make a copy of the "Freckles the Fish" worksheet for each child. Have the children color their fish and cut them out. Tie the fish at various lengths from a wooden dowel. Tie or position the dowel where the fish can "swim" around. Or, if you have string lines for hanging decorations, tie the fish on the lines and your classroom will look like an aquarium!

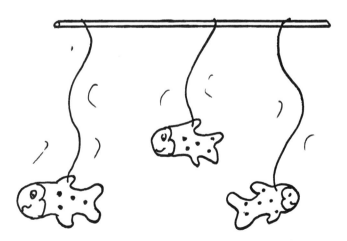

Caught Napping

Make a Freckles fishing game. Make a copy of the "Freckles the Fish" worksheet for each child. Have each child color a fish and cut it out. Write their name on the back of the fish. Tape a paper clip to the front of the fish near its mouth. Attach a string to a dowel and a magnet at the opposite end to make a fishing rod. Lay all the fish on the floor, name-side down. Let each child take a turn fishing. When each fish is caught, hold up the name and say, "Sarah caught Jason napping!"

Poinsettia

Poinsettia plants abound in December. Their beautiful red leaves add a burst of color to wintry days. The poinsettia is really a shrub that grows to 10 feet tall in very warm climates. The leaves at the top of the poinsettia are red; the ones behind or below the red ones are green. The real flowers of the poinsettia are the little yellow blossoms that are clustered in the middle of the red leaves. (Mention to the children that the plants also come in white.)

Make a copy of the "Poinsettia" worksheet for each child. Say, "Color this poinsettia. Remember, the little blossoms in the middle are yellow. The top leaves are red; these have an R on them. The bottom leaves are green; these have a G on them. You can cut out your poinsettia and glue it onto a piece of folded construction paper to make a holiday greeting card."

Carrot Nose

Make a copy of the "Carrot Nose" worksheet for each child. Help the children with the directions, if necessary.

Help Santa Fill the Stocking

Make a copy of the "Help Santa Fill the Stocking" worksheet for each child. Say, "Color the stocking and the toys, then cut out each. Glue the toys onto the stocking."

Santa's Moose

Make a copy of the "Santa's Moose" worksheet for each child. Say, "Make your own moose to help Santa on Christmas Eve. Color your moose's eyes and nostrils. Color his head lightly with your brown crayon. Cut out his head. Glue the head on the bottom half of a piece of 9" × 12" construction paper. Trace your hands on top of your moose's head to make antlers. Color the antlers.

Be sure to read *Santa's Moose* (See "December Storytime").

D Is for Drum

Make a copy of the "D Is for Drum" worksheet for each child. Have the children color the drum. Then have the children make a drumstick by sticking a small ball of clay onto the end of a craft stick or pencil. They can pretend they're playing along to a marching record or to the *Little Drummer Boy* song.

Santa Bag Puppet

You will need lunch-sized paper bags, scissors, crayons or markers, and glue. Make a copy of the "Santa Bag Puppet" worksheet for each child. Have the children color Santa and then cut him out. Glue Santa's head onto the bottom flap of the paper bag. Fold the flap up and glue his body to the bag. The children can place their fingers in the flap of the bag to make the bag puppet move.

Rocky the Rocking Horse

Make a copy of the "Rocky the Rocking Horse" worksheet for each child. Let the children use crayons or markers to color Rocky. They can also color the circle or decorate it with stripes or dots. Let the children cut out their circles, while you cut out each child's Rocky. Have the children fold the circle in half, and then cut Rocky's legs along the dotted lines. The children can glue Rocky onto the circle, with one front leg on each side of the circle, and one back leg on each side of the circle. Gently rock him back and forth. Have the children be rocking horses themselves—they can stand with hands on hips, legs apart, and rock side to side.

A December Color Book

Make a copy of the "December Color Book" for each child. The children can color each page, and then cut the pages apart along the black lines. Staple the book in the top left corner.

Santa's Bag

Make a copy of the "Santa's Bag" worksheet. It deals with the concepts of *little, medium,* and *big.* Help the children with directions, if necessary.

Here Comes Winter

Discuss with the children the changes they will see and feel as winter weather arrives. (Of course, if you live in a warm climate all year-long, you can discuss what those particular changes will be and show pictures.)

Make a "Here Comes Winter" bulletin board display or mural. Give the children department store flyers, ski equipment catalogs, winter festival announcements, and various other winter mailings. Have the children look for—and cut out—winter clothes, sporting activities, snow scenes, etc. Glue these onto a large piece of kraft paper or colored background paper. Add cotton for snow.

Holiday Gift Wrap

You will need plain paper, a small piece of sponge or half a raw potato with a design cut into it, small paper plates, and tempera paints.

Pour a small amount of paint onto each plate, and dip the sponge or potato half into a dish of paint. Have the children print their designs by pressing the sponge or potato over and over again on the paper. If you include smaller paper in this activity, they can make matching gift cards as well.

The children can use the gift wrap and cards for presents to give to friends and family for Hanukkah and Christmas.

Jingle Bells

Make a jingle bell chain. Make a copy of the "Jingle Bells" worksheet for each child. Color the bells gold (yellow) or silver (gray). Color the holes at the bottom of the bells black. Help the children, if necessary, to cut out the bells. Use a hole punch to make a hole at the top of each bell. String the bells with yarn and knot the bells. (Put the large bell in the middle.)

——————————— MUSIC AND MOVEMENT ———————————

Five Little Reindeer Jumping on the Bed

You can use this activity with any season or animal. Have five children at a time stand in a line. Everyone sings the following:

Five little reindeer jumping on the bed (*jump up and down*)
One fell off and bumped its head. (*teacher points to one child who "falls" and puts hand on head*)

Momma calls the doctor and the doctor said (*make dialing motion*)
"No more reindeer jumping on the bed." (*shake finger*)
***
Four little reindeer jumping on the bed (*jump up and down*)
One fell off and bumped its head (*teacher points to one child who "falls" and puts hand on head*)
Momma calls the doctor and the doctor said (*make dialing motion*)
"No more reindeer jumping on the bed." (*shake finger*)
***
Three little reindeer jumping on the bed (*jump up and down*)
One fell off and bumped its head (*teacher points to one child who "falls" and puts hand on head*)
Momma calls the doctor and the doctor said (*make dialing motion*)
"No more reindeer jumping on the bed." (*shake finger*)
***
Two little reindeer jumping on the bed (*jump up and down*)
One fell off and bumped its head (*teacher points to one child who "falls" and puts hand on head*)
Momma calls the doctor and the doctor said (*make dialing motion*)
"No more reindeer jumping on the bed." (*shake finger*)
***

One little reindeer jumping on the bed (*jump up and down*)
This one fell off and bumped its head (*teacher points to remaining child who "falls" and puts hand on head*)
Momma calls the doctor and the doctor said (*make dialing motion*)
"No more reindeer jumping on the bed." (*shake finger*)

Two Little Feet

Two little feet go tap, tap, tap.
Two little hands go clap, clap, clap.
One little body turns around.
One little child quietly sits down.

A Listening Game

Have the children turn their backs while you make various sounds for them to guess. Some examples of sounds are: crumbling a piece of paper, clapping hands, blowing a whistle, tapping on a wooden desk, writing on a chalkboard, rubbing two blocks together, and tapping on the window.

Variations: 1. Have children guess what rhythm band instrument you are playing. 2. Place pictures of a train, dog, phone, etc., on the chalkboard ledge. Say the sound that each picture represents. Have the children point to the picture.

SONGS, POEMS, AND FINGERPLAYS

A Fish Ditty

Five little fishes
In an itsy bitsy brook.
"Swim," said their mother.
"Swim if you can."
So they swam and they swam
All over the dam.

Hands on Shoulders

Have the children do the appropriate actions while saying the following:

Hands on shoulders, hands on knees,
Hands behind you, if you please.
Touch your hair,
Now your toes.
Hands up high in the air.
Down at your sides, now touch your hair.
Hands up high, as before.
Now clap your hands, one, two, three, four!

Jack in the Box

Jack in the box (*close hand with thumb inside*)
You sit so still.
Won't you come out?
Yes, I will! (*pop thumb out*)

Little Red Caboose

Little red caboose, little red caboose,
Little red caboose behind the train.
Smoke stack on its back, back, back (*pat back 3 times*)
Riding down the track, track, track (*bend elbows and move arms forward and back*)
Little red caboose behind the train,
Choo, choo! (*make up-and-down pulling motion*)

FROM BUTTON'S COUNTRY KITCHEN

Matzoh Balls

2 eggs, lightly beaten	1 quart boiling water
2 tablespoons vegetable oil	3 chicken bouillon cubes
½ cup matzoh meal	dash of salt and pepper

Mix the eggs, oil, salt and pepper. Gradually add the matzoh meal. Stir until thick. Refrigerate for 20 minutes in a covered bowl. Then form the dough into golf ball-sized balls. Dissolve the bouillon cubes in boiling water. Drop the matzoh balls into the water and simmer for 30 minutes. Drain and serve.

Penny Punch

1 3–ounce package cherry gelatin	2 cups cold water
1 3–ounce package lemon gelatin	1 orange, thinly sliced
2 cups boiling water	1 28–ounce bottle ginger ale

Dissolve the gelatin in boiling water. Add cold water and the orange slices. Chill. Then add ginger ale (and ice cubes, if desired) just before serving. Makes 2 quarts.

Glue Cookies

Put ½ cup of light corn syrup into a saucepan. Mix in ½ cup sugar. Heat and mix until boiling. Remove from heat and add ½ cup peanut butter and 3 cups of corn flakes. Spread the mixture evenly into a flat, greased cookie sheet. Let the mixture cool and then cut into squares.

VIDEOS FOR DECEMBER

Rudolph the Red-Nosed Reindeer (Broadway Video, Videocraft International, Ltd., 1968)

Christmas is in jeopardy of being cancelled because of a fierce blizzard. Rudolph's glowing nose saves the day by guiding Santa around the world. Approximate running time: 53 minutes.

After viewing this video, have the children make the "Rudolph Mobile" in the readiness section.

Frosty the Snowman (Broadway Video, Videocraft International, Ltd., 1969)

An American classic, Frosty comes to life and experiences a storm of adventures. He outwits the dastardly plans of an evil magician and finds safety and happiness at the North Pole. Approximate running time: 30 minutes.

This video goes well with the "Carrot Nose" activity and the melting snow (or ice cubes) lesson.

The Little Drummer Boy (Broadway Video, Videocraft International, Ltd., 1968)

This touching story is about a young, orphaned drummer boy who escapes from his kidnapper and begins a search for his camel. He finds his animal in the manger. Having no gift for the newborn baby, the drummer boy plays a song on his drum to the delight of the special baby. Approximate running time: 30 minutes.

A discussion about gifts-from-the-heart and the making of the "D Is for Drum" project are good follow-ups to this video.

WORKSHEETS FOR DECEMBER

The following worksheets are referred to in this month's readiness activities.

"I Care and Share" Medallion

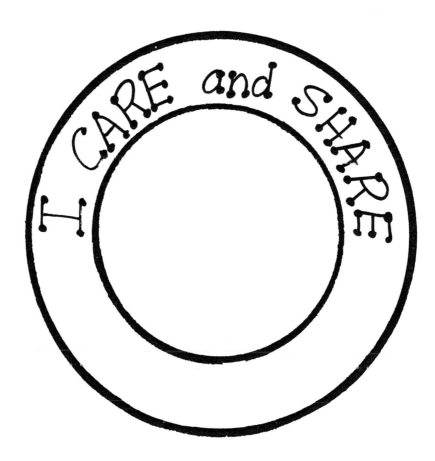

This is a nice project to make after reading the story *The Berenstain Bears Meet Santa Bear* (December Storytime), and/or after a discussion about being nice to each other.

Photocopy as many medallions as you need. Glue them on cardboard or oaktag and cut them out. With markers, have each child drawn their face in the circle. Punch a hole in the top of the medallion and string it with yarn. Present each child with their medallion and a big "I'm proud of YOU."

Triangle Tree

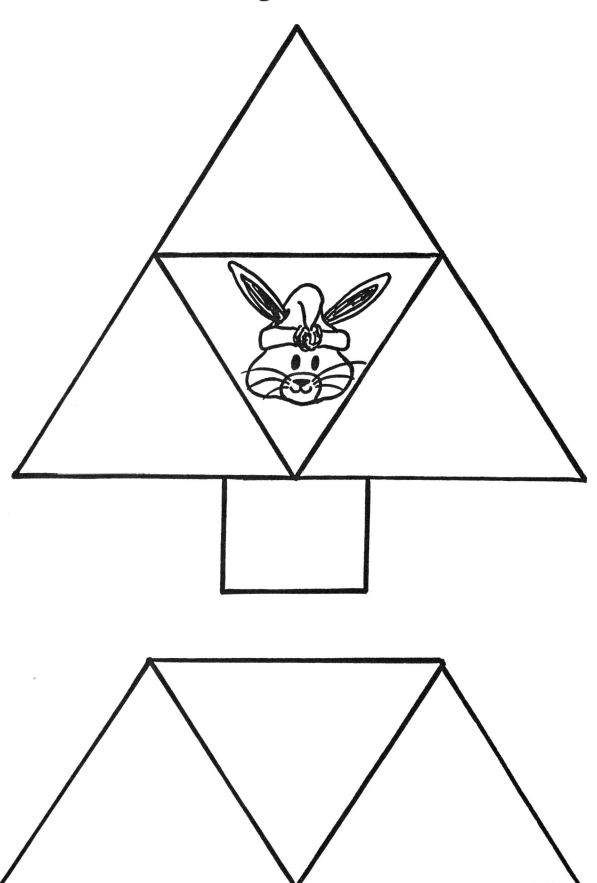

P. J. The Christmas Bear

Dreidel Chain

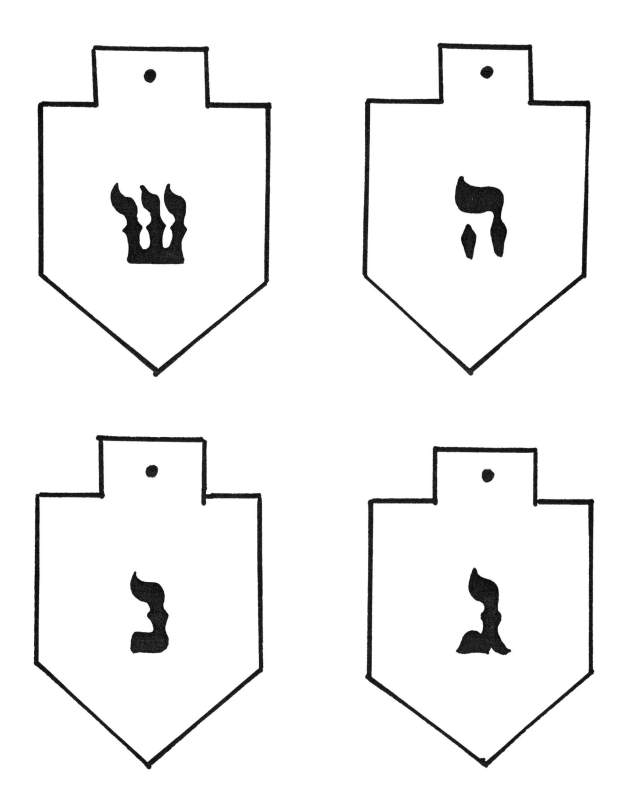

Rudolph Mobile

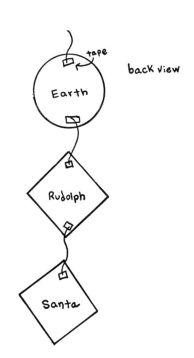

Worms like to sleep through the winter under rocks. Can you draw a worm? Sure you can. He's only a squiggly line! Try it. Go over this worm. Then make a few of your own.

Now go over the numbers below. Color these rocks lightly with your gray crayon. Draw the correct number of worms under each rock. Use a different color for each worm.

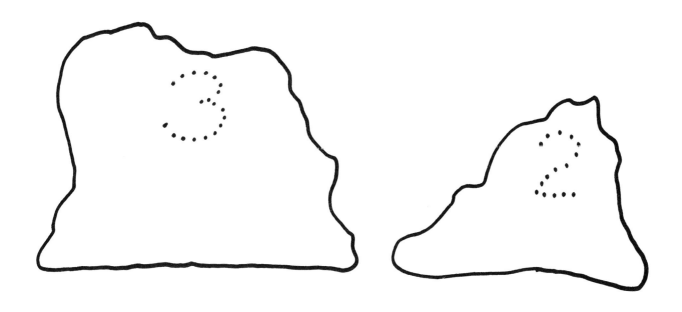

Hibernating Fish

Reddy the Robin

Freckles the Fish

Poinsettia

Carrot Nose

Connect the dots to find out who has a carrot for a nose.

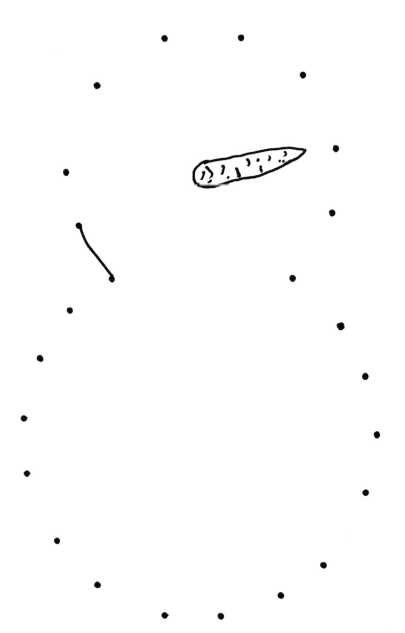

Color the carrot orange. Give the snowman eyes, a mouth, and buttons. Draw two brown sticks for arms. Can you draw a hat on the snowman's head?

Help Santa Fill the Stocking

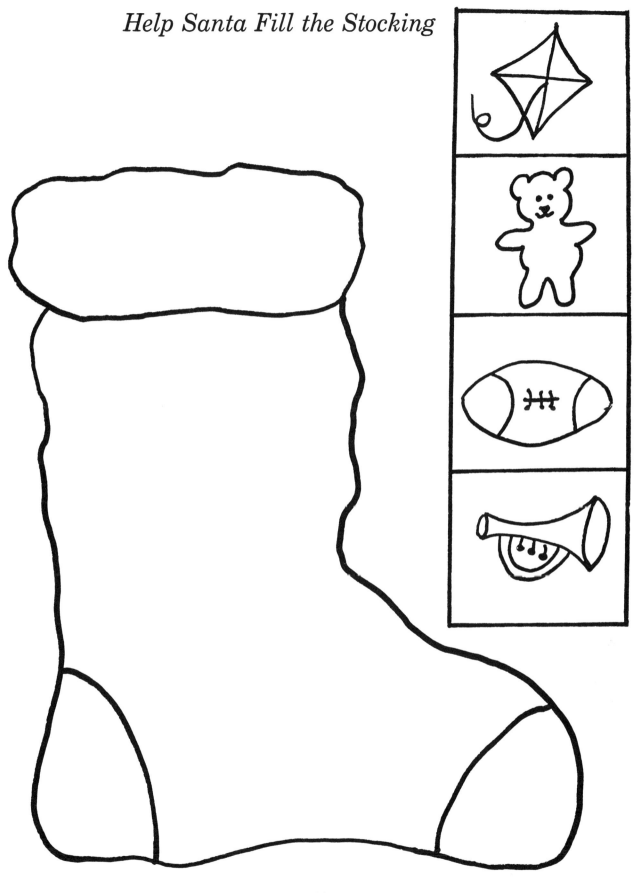

Santa's Moose

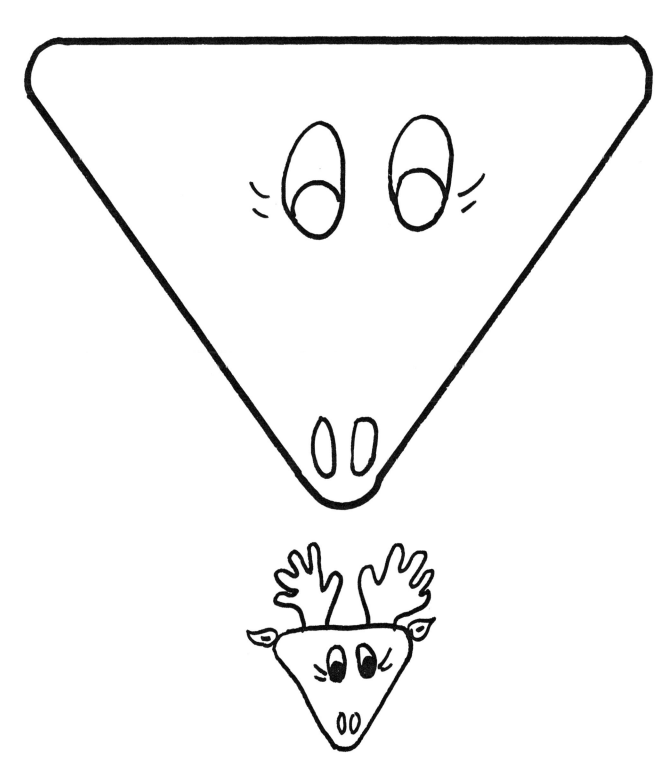

D Is for Drum

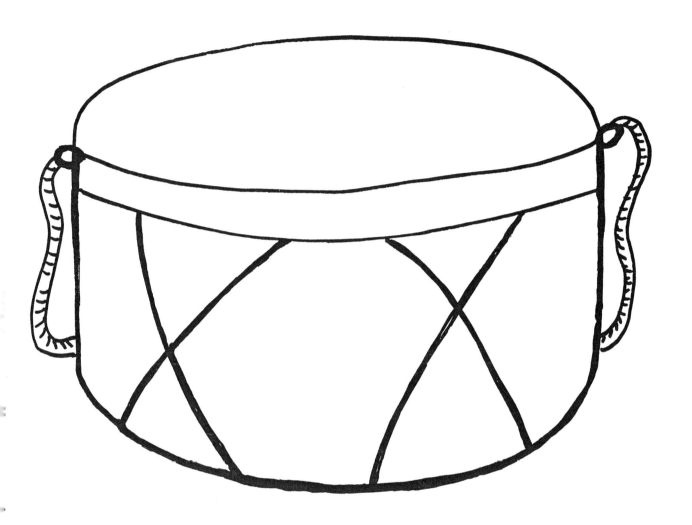

Santa Bag Puppet

142

Santa Bag Puppet (continued)

Rocky the Rocking Horse

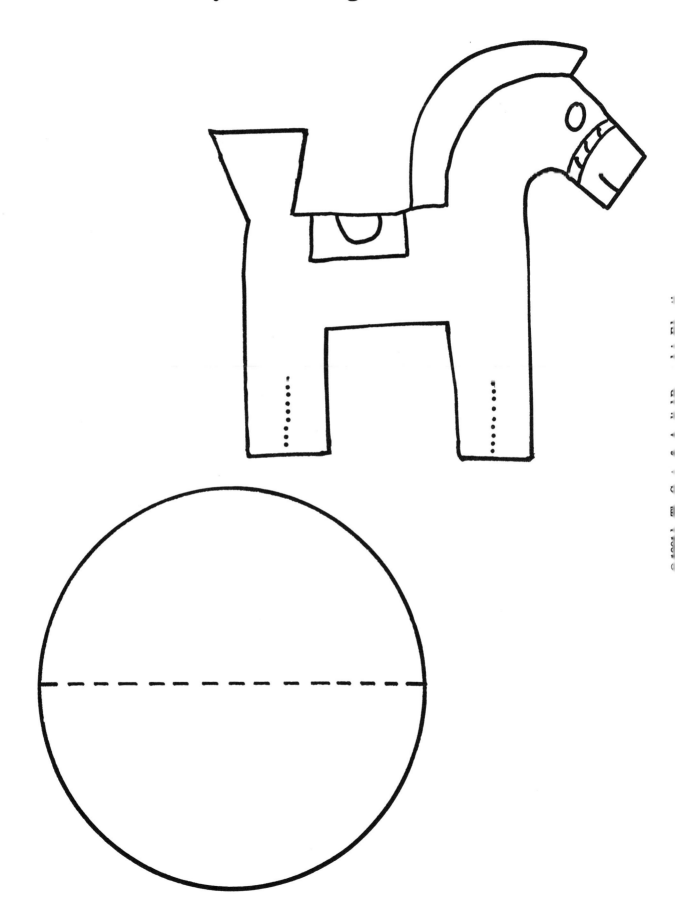

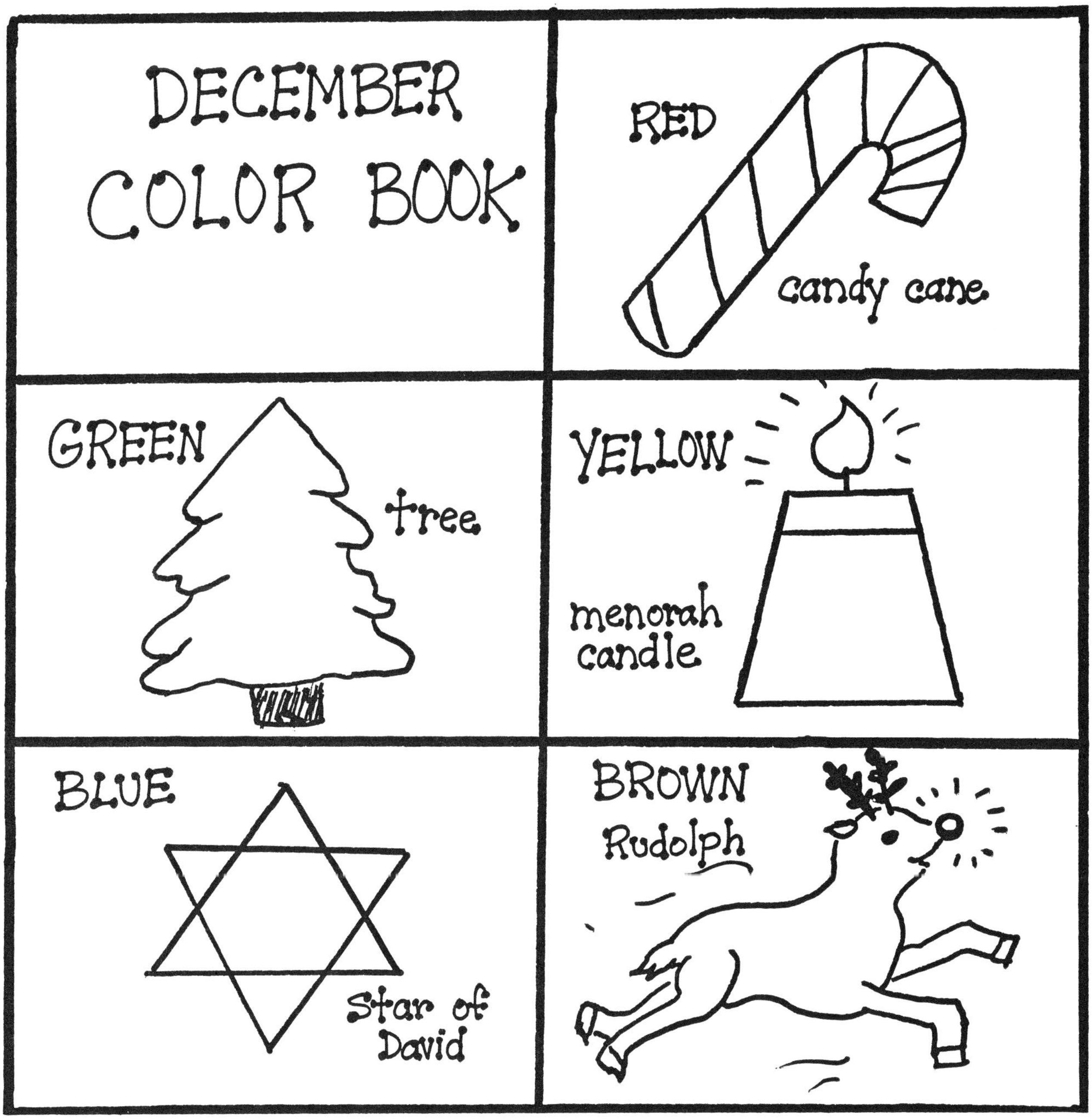

DECEMBER COLOR BOOK

RED

candy cane

GREEN tree

YELLOW

menorah candle

BLUE

Star of David

BROWN Rudolph

Santa's Bag

Put your finger on the LITTLE ball. Color it blue. Put your finger on the MEDIUM-sized ball. Color it red. Put your finger on the BIG ball. Color it yellow.

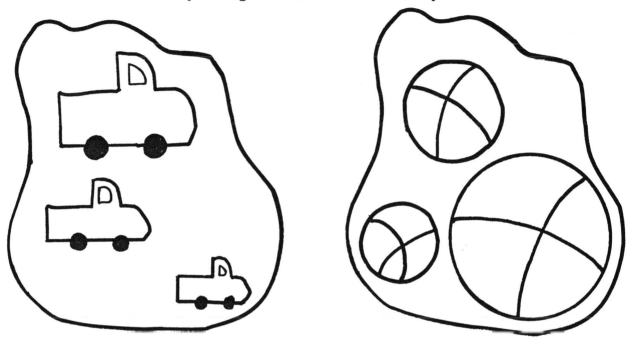

Put your finger on the BIG truck. Color it green. Put your finger on the MEDIUM-sized truck. Color it purple. Put your finger on the LITTLE truck. Color it brown.

Put your finger on the MEDIUM-sized bear. Color it red. Put your finger on the LITTLE bear. Color it orange. Put your finger on the BIG bear. Color it blue.

Jingle Bells

January—A Good Month For Dinosaurs!

The holidays are over, but not the learning and fun in preschool. Dinosaurs are the theme for this month. The children quickly learn the names of the dinosaurs (if they don't know them already) and their characteristics. Set up a dinosaur display table and invite the children to bring in their dinosaur memorabilia. Depending on the fine motor skills of your children, you may want to do some of the cutting on these projects. The projects may be traced onto oaktag to make them sturdier.

Beginnings

Dear Parents:

You'll be hearing some new, long vocabulary words from your pre-schoolers this month—we're discussing dinosaurs! Our math, social studies, and science readiness projects will all relate to these giant prehistoric creatures. We'll be looking at pictures of dinosaurs and making our own.

Join in our fun by asking your child to tell you about these fascinating creatures. At the end of the month, we're going to put on a dinosaur play.

Sincerely,

_____

Your children will meet some wonderful dinosaurs in the following books.

Danny and the Dinosaur by SYD HOFF (Harper & Brothers)

Danny meets a real, live dinosaur in the museum. They spend a delightful day together exploring the city and playing with Danny's friends. At day's end, the dinosaur returns to his home in the museum and Danny, sadly, to his home. "But we did have a wonderful day," they say.

The Big-Little Dinosaur by DARLENE GEIS (Wonder Books—Price/Stern/Sloan)

Danny, a baby brontosaurus, sets out to find his family. He encounters many different kinds of dinosaurs before he happily finds his family.

Tyrannosaurus Was a Beast by JACK PRETULSKY (Greenwillow Books)

The drawings are wonderful, and the book is sure to make you and your children laugh.

The News About Dinosaurs by PATRICIA LAUBER (Bradbury Press)

This is a nonfiction book with magnificent drawings and paintings. The author presents different ideas about the colors of dinosaurs, about whether or not they had feathers, and so on. The children will be sure to want to flip through the pages.

Big Old Bones—A Dinosaur Tale by CAROL CARRICK (Clarion Books, Houghton-Mifflin Co.)

Professor Potts is out West on vacation. He discovers some big, old bones and brings them back East to reassemble. After many attempts, Professor Potts finally assembles a Tribrontosaurus Rex!

Flying Dragons by DAVID ELDRIDGE (Troll Associates)

This nonfiction book has very graphic pictures of the many kinds of flying reptiles that lived in ancient times. It gives interesting facts about their daily survival habits and ultimate demise.

Snow by ROY MCKEE AND P. D. EASTMAN (Beginner Books, a division of Random House)

Two young children thoroughly enjoy the new fallen snow. They sled, ski, make a snow house, and build the biggest snowman in town. When the hot sun melts the snow, the children gather some snowballs to store in the freezer for another day's fun.

Share this story with your children as a change of pace from dinosaurs, especially if you live in an area that gets snow. You and your children might even make snowballs and keep them in a freezer; then experiment with their melting.

Poppy the Panda by DICK GACKENBACH (Clarion Books)

Katie O'Keefe has a toy panda that refuses to go to sleep one night because it has nothing to wear. Katie makes amusing attempts to solve Poppy's problem. This is a charming story to read before the children do the "P Is for Panda" activity described later.

—————— READINESS ACTIVITIES FOR JANUARY ——————

Stone Footprints

The word dinosaur means "terrible lizard." Once dinosaurs ruled the earth. There are no dinosaurs now, but we know from bones found and footprints discovered in stone that these creatures roamed the earth around 150 million years ago.

With your children, look at dinosaur footprints in an encyclopedia or dinosaur book. Help the children make their own stone footprints using this recipe for salt dough:

You will need 4 cups of flour, 1 cup of salt, 1 tablespoon of oil, and 1½ cups of water. Mix these together and knead the dough until smooth.

Flatten out a piece of dough sufficient for a child's footprint. Put a piece of aluminum foil on the floor, then the dough, then a piece of plastic wrap. Have the child press his or her bare foot into the dough. Set the dough on a windowsill to dry.

Which Dinosaur Is It?

Make a copy of the "Which Dinosaur Is It?" worksheet for each student. Say, "Start at number one and continue to number ten to complete this three-horned dinosaur. What is its name? (Triceratops) Now color the dinosaur."

How Big Is a "Thunder Lizard"?

The brontosaurus was a huge dinosaur—about 80 feet long. Measure 80 feet of string. Take the children into the hall, gym, or outside. Have one child hold one end of the string, then walk with the rest of the class until the string is stretched. Can they imagine an animal *that* long?

Dinosaur Eggs

All dinosaurs hatched from eggs. The first eggs that scientists found were from Protoceratops dinosaurs. The mother dinosaur laid her eggs in the sand. She did not sit on the eggs like a chicken does. She was too heavy for that! The sun warmed her eggs. The babies were small, about the size of a rabbit.

Make a copy of the "Dinosaur Eggs" worksheet for each student. Say, "Color the dinosaur eggs and cut them out. Color the sand nest yellow. Then glue the eggs onto the nest."

The "Flying Dragon"

While the dinosaurs roamed the earth, the prehistoric skies were filled with many different kinds of pterosaurs, or "flying dragons." The ancient seas were shallow, warm, and filled with fish. The flying dragons spent their days diving for fish.

Make a copy of the "Flying Dragon" worksheet for each child. Say, "Color this flying dragon. Cut it out. Tie a 12–inch piece of string or yarn at each X. (Put a piece of tape over the X to make it more rip-resistant.) Hold the string and run to make your pterosaurs swoop. Be sure to run in a safe place!"

Triceratops

This dinosaur's skin was as thick and hard as armor. It was about as big as a car. Triceratops, which means "three horns on the face," used its three sharp horns to protect itself from the bigger dinosaurs.

Make a copy of the "Triceratops" worksheet for each student. Say, "Color the triceratops' parts and cut them out. Cut the slits in its body and insert its legs. Glue on the tail. When the Triceratops has its horns down, it's ready for danger!"

Brontosaurus

This dinosaur was longer than a trailer truck and very heavy. It was so heavy that scientists believe that every step it took shook the ground. Because of this, Brontosaurus is called the "thunder lizard."

Make a copy of the "Brontosaurus" worksheet for each student. Say, "Color your Brontosaurus' parts and cut them out. Fold the legs on the dotted lines. Cut the slits on the body and insert the legs. The small legs go in front; the large legs in back. Glue on its tail. Make your thunder lizard walk around and shake the earth!"

Tyrannosaurus Rex

Tyrannosaurus Rex, "King of the Tyrants," was the most terrible dinosaur that ever lived. It stood on its strong hind legs and had small front legs. Tyrannosaurus Rex was taller than a house and 50 feet long. It had a powerful jaw with teeth that were 6 inches long. Tyrannosaurus Rex could eat almost any other dinosaur.

Make a copy of the "Tyrannosaurus Rex" worksheet for each child. Say, "Color 'the King' and cut out all the pieces. Cut the slit in its body and insert the legs. Glue on the tail. Tell the other dinosaurs to behave—the 'King' has arrived!"

Stegosaurus Puzzle

Stegosaurus, which means "covered lizard," had large pointed plates on its back. On its tail were four long sharp spikes. The Stegosaurus had a very small head, with a brain the size of a walnut.

Make a copy of the "Stegosaurus Puzzle" worksheet for each student. Say, "Color the Stegosaurus and go over the letters of its name. Glue the Stegosaurus onto a piece of oaktag and cut it into four or five pieces. Mix up the pieces, and then put the Stegosaurus back together."

Going for a Swim

The duckbill dinosaurs spent most of their time in the water. Make a copy of the "Duckbill Dinosaur" worksheet for each student. Have the children color their picture with crayons. Then help them make a wash of one-half teaspoon blue paint and one-half cup water. Brush the wash over the entire picture. The crayoned dinosaur will "resist" the water.

Which Is Longer?

Use an opaque projector to enlarge the following two dinosaurs on the wall or screen. Ask the students to tell you which dinosaur they think is longer.

Which Is Taller?

Use an opaque projector to enlarge the following two dinosaurs on the wall or screen. Ask the children to tell you which dinosaur they think is taller.

Additional Dinosaur Activities

● There are many good dinosaur cassettes and records in teachers' supplies catalogs. They contain dinosaur sounds, songs, and activities. You could have a prehistoric parade!

- Have a Fossil Hunt in a sandbox. Make some fossil bones from oaktag or construction paper. Hide them in the sand for the children to find. Or, hide the bones around the classroom or play area.
- Take a field trip to a museum and view a dinosaur exhibit.
- From a roll of kraft paper, make a giant dinosaur footprint. Trace each child's foot on it, and hang the giant footprint on the wall.
- Have the children make a dinosaur's sand nest in the sandbox. Use playground balls for eggs.
- Obtain an inflatable prehistoric animal globe and have a game of catch.
- Play the game "Hot Potato" with an oaktag dinosaur bone or soft rubber dog bone. Use a dinosaur record or cassette for music.
- Make a dinosaur train. Collect cardboard boxes (the ones that 2–liter soda bottles come in are perfect). Cut out the tops and bottoms of the boxes. Then have the children paint the boxes to resemble a dinosaur. Add a tail to the last box. Have a child stand inside each box. Show the children how to hold the box up under their arms. The dinosaur train is ready to roll!

Number Soup

Make a copy of the "Number Soup" worksheet for each child. Say, "Find all the ones in the soup. Circle them with your red crayon. Find all the twos. Circle them with your green crayon. Find all the threes in the soup. Circle them with your orange crayon. Now color the soup yellow. Color the spoon and the bowl in your favorite colors. Cut out the bowl of soup and glue it on a paper plate. Cut out the spoon. Make believe you're eating number soup."

P Is for Panda

After reading *Poppy the Panda* (see "January Storytime"), the children can make a panda of their own.

Make a copy of the "P Is for Panda" worksheet for each child. Say, "With your black marker or crayon, color the panda's eyes, nose, and ears. (Don't color over the eyeballs.) Cut out all the pieces. Glue the eyes, nose, and ears onto the panda's head as shown. Draw a little mouth with your red marker or crayon. Glue on a bow made from yarn or ribbon."

The ABC Cats

Make a copy of "The ABC Cats" worksheet for each student. Say, "These three cats love milk. Help Abe, Bonnie, and Carl find their own saucers of milk. Draw a line from each cat to its saucer of milk. Then color the cats."

Ice Cream for You and a Friend

Make a copy of the "Ice Cream Cones" worksheet for each child. Say, "Follow the numbers with your marker or crayon, starting with number one. Color the cones yellow or light brown. Color your ice cream in your favorite flavor. Ask what your friend's favorite flavor is and then color that cone. Cut out the two ice cream cones. Give a cone to your friend. Pretend to take a big lick!"

Who's Missing?

This is a detail-awareness game. Have all the children sit on the floor. Turn a chair with its back to the children. Choose one child to sit in the chair and close his or her eyes. Point to another child sitting on the floor. This child quietly leaves the room. The rest of the children say, "Someone's leaving preschool and (name of child in chair) doesn't know who it is. Turn around!" The child in the chair turns around and tries to guess "who's missing." The class can give clues: It's a boy. He has on a red shirt today. His name starts with P. He's the Calendar Person. And so on. When the child guesses "who's missing," the child outside the room returns and sits in the chair. The game is repeated until everyone has had a chance.

Dr. Martin Luther King, Jr.

On January 20, we honor the late black civil rights leader, Dr. Martin Luther King, Jr. Dr. King believed in equal rights for all people. He struggled in a peaceful manner to achieve his dream.

Make a copy of the "Mobile" worksheet for each child. The students will make this mobile as a reminder of the wonderful dream Dr. King had for America. Have the children go over the letters with their yellow, orange, or any other light-colored marker. Help the children to cut out the pieces, and to string and tape them as shown here.

Snowflakes

Make a copy of the "Snowflakes" worksheet for each child. Say, "Most snowflakes are crystals with six rays. Start at number one and count the rays of these snowflakes. To make your snowflakes sparkle, put lines of glue on the six rays. Sprinkle them with glitter or colored sugar. Shake off the excess." (If you have the children make snowflakes on dark colored construction paper, use salt or white sugar instead of glitter.)

Snowballs

Make a copy of the "Snowballs" worksheet for each student. Say, "How many snowballs are there in each pile? Count the snowballs, and then go over the numeral."

Build an Ice House

Make a copy of the "Ice House" worksheet for each student. Say, "Cut out the rectangles on the solid black line. Then cut on all the dotted lines so that you have six rectangles. On a piece of construction paper, make these rectangles into an ice house like the one shown. Glue them in place. Now draw yourself in the ice house!"

January Mittens

Make a copy of the "January Mittens" worksheet for each child. Say, "Be creative! Color these mittens with stripes, dots, however you want. Then cut out the mittens and string them with yarn as shown."

Make a Snowman

Make a copy of the "Make a Snowman" worksheet for each child. Say, "Here are three snowballs. Cut them out. Find the biggest one and glue it near the bottom of a piece of construction paper. Now find the medium-sized snowball and glue it on top of the big one. Glue the smallest snowball on top of the medium-sized snowball. With your black marker, give your snowman a hat, eyes, nose, mouth, and buttons. With your brown marker, give the snowman stick arms."

Mitten Match

Make a copy of the "Mitten Match" worksheet for each student. Say, "Cut off the strip of mittens on the right. Then cut the strip into single mittens. Count the dots on the mittens at the left, and place the correct numbered mitten next to it. Continue to match the mittens. Now mix up the mittens. Make a pile of the numeral mittens and put a paper clip on them. Take this activity home and do the matching for someone at home."

MUSIC AND MOVEMENT

Miss Snowflake

I watched little Miss Snowflake as she floated down. (*float hands down*)
I saw her 'round and 'round. (*turn around*)
She drifted up. She drifted down. (*move arms up; move arms down*)
And then she fell upon the ground. (*sit on floor*)

If You're Happy and You Know It

If you're happy and you know it, clap your hands (*clap, clap*)
If you're happy and you know it, clap your hands (*clap, clap*)
If you're happy and you know it, then your face will surely show it,
If you're happy and you know it, clap your hands (*clap, clap*)

If you're angry and you know it, stomp your feet (*stomp, stomp*)
If you're angry and you know it, stomp your feet (*stomp, stomp*)
If you're angry and you know it, then your face will surely show it.
If you're angry and you know it, stomp your feet (*stomp, stomp*)

If you're tired and you know it, go to sleep (*close eyes*)
If you're tired and you know it, go to sleep (*close eyes*)
If you're tired and you know it, then your face will surely show it.
If you're tired and you know it, go to sleep (*close eyes*)

The Scale Song

(DO)   DOE   (a deer, a female deer)
(RE)   RAY   (a drop of golden sun)
(MI)   ME   (a name I call myself)
(FA)   FAR   (a long, long way to run)
(SO)   SEW   (a needle pulling thread)
(LA)   LA   (a note to follow sew)
(TI)   TEA   (a drink with jam and bread)
       That will bring us back to DOE!

Playing Prehistorics

Here's a play for 13 children. You can easily add or subtract lines if you have more or fewer students.

Child 1:   Hi dinosaurs! What are your names?
Child 2:   We are all Brontosaurus dinosaurs.
Child 3:   We are giant-size dinosaurs.
Child 4:   When we walk the ground shakes.
Child 5:   We sound like thunder. Listen! (*One of the children plays a drum and all the Brontosaurus' plod out*)
           Enter four more dinosaurs.
Child 1:   Hi dinosaurs! What are your names?
Child 6:   We are all Stegosaurus dinosaurs.
Child 7:   We have large plates on our backs. (*Pats back*)
Child 8:   We have 4 sharp spikes on our tails. (*Extends arm and puts up four fingers*)
Child 9:   Our brains are only the size of a walnut. (*Child makes a circle with his/her forefinger and thumb*)

Children exit swishing extended arm with four fingers in the air.
Enter four more dinosaurs.

Child 1: Hi dinosaurs! What are your names?

Child 10: We are all Tyrannosaurus Rex dinosaurs.

Child 11: We are the Kings of the dinosaurs.

Child 12: Everyone is afraid of us.
We are as tall as a house.

Child 13: We are going out for a dinosaur dinner tonight. Do you want to come?

Child 1: NO THANKS! (*Exits*)

Tyrannosaurus' shake each others' hands and exit.

—————— SONGS, POEMS, and FINGERPLAYS ——————

Dinosaurs, We Love You

Sing this song to the tune of *Frere Jacques:*

Stegasaurus, Stegasaurus
We love you
We love you
You have spikes on your tail
You have spikes on your tail
Goodbye to you
Goodbye to you
****

Brontosaurus, Brontosaurus
We love you
We love you
It thunders when you walk
It thunders when you walk
Goodbye to you
Goodbye to you
****

Pterodactyl, Pterodactyl
We love you
We love you
You fly up in the sky
You fly up in the sky
Goodbye to you
Goodbye to you
****

Triceratop, Triceratop
We love you
We love you
You have horns on your head

You have horns on your head
Goodbye to you
Goodbye to you
                    ****
Duckbill dinosaur, Duckbill dinosaur
We love you
We love you
You swim in the water
You swim in the water
Goodbye to you
Goodbye to you

FROM BUTTON'S COUNTRY KITCHEN

Bread Pudding

8 slices of bread   3 eggs
¼ cup soft margarine   ¼ teaspoon salt
½ cup sugar   4 cups milk

Preheat the oven to 300°F. Grease a baking dish. Trim the crusts from the bread. Spread margarine on both sides of the bread and place in the baking dish. In a bowl, beat the sugar and eggs until creamy. Add the salt and milk. Pour over the bread in the baking dish and let stand for 15 minutes. Then bake for one hour. Cover the dish for the first 30 minutes of baking.

Peanut Butter Bread

2 cups flour   1 egg, beaten
2 teaspoons baking powder   1 cup milk
1 teaspoon salt   butter or margarine for greasing
⅓ cup sugar   the loaf pan
¾ cup peanut butter

Preheat the oven to 350°F. Grease a loaf pan. In a large bowl, mix together the flour, baking powder, salt, and sugar. With a fork, work in the peanut butter. Add the beaten egg and milk. Pour into the greased loaf pan and bake for 1 hour.

VIDEOS FOR JANUARY

Mister Rogers Home Video: Dinosaurs and Monsters (Family Communications, 1986)

Monsters of fact and fantasy are the subject of this video. Mister Rogers talks and sings about important childhood feelings. Approximate running time: 64 minutes.

Digging up Dinosaurs (Children's Video Library, 1989)

This video is appropriate for children ages 4 and up. From the award-winning series *Reading Rainbow,* this video takes us back in time to explore the mysteries surrounding the life and death of dinosaurs. Approximate running time: 30 minutes.

Dinosaurs, Dinosaurs, Dinosaurs (Twin Tower Enterprises, Inc., 1987)

This entertaining and educational video begins with the video's host, Gary Owens, who thinks that he is turning into a dinosaur! This acclaimed program will fascinate and intrigue the children. Approximate running time: 30 minutes.

——————— WORKSHEETS FOR JANUARY ———————

The following worksheets are referred to in this month's readiness activities.

Which Dinosaur Is It?

5

4

3

2

1

Dinosaur Eggs

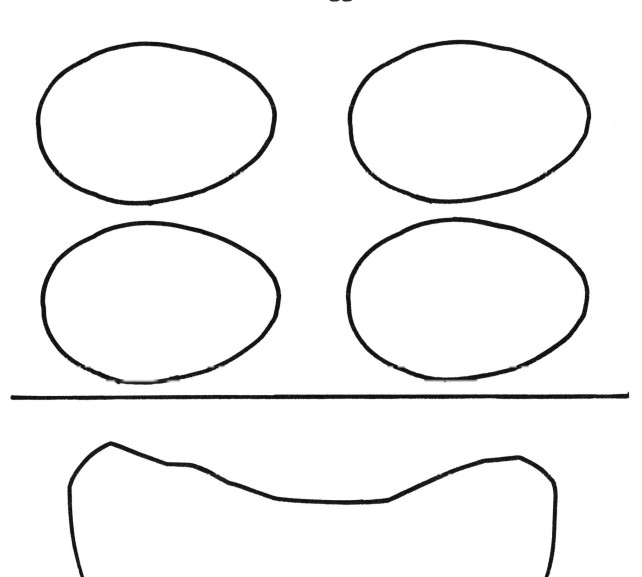

Flying Dragon

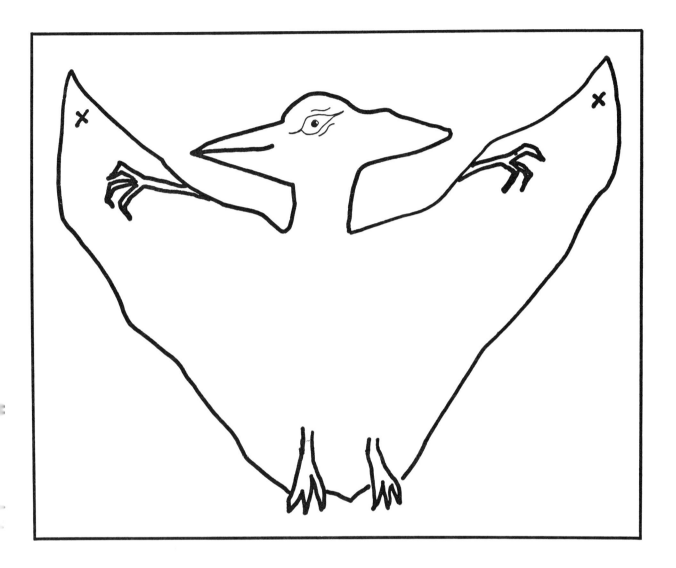

Triceratops

fold

166

Brontosaurus

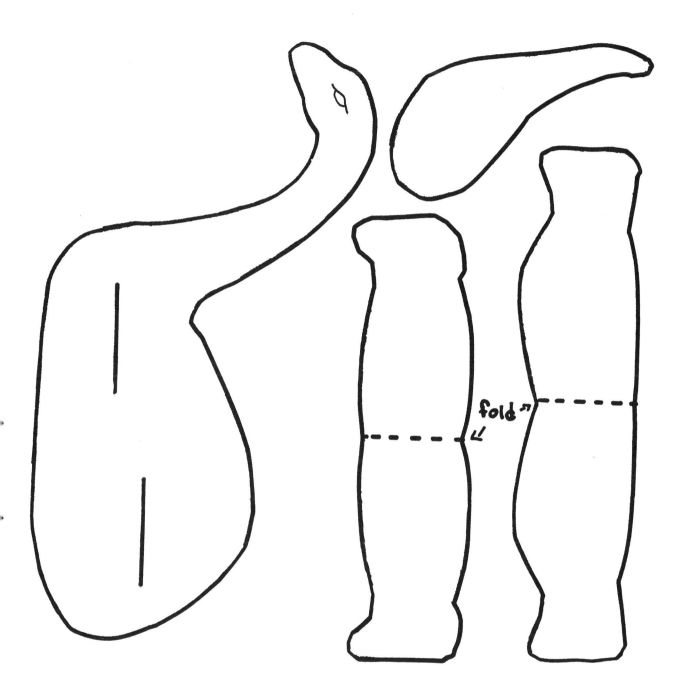

fold

Tyrannosaurus Rex

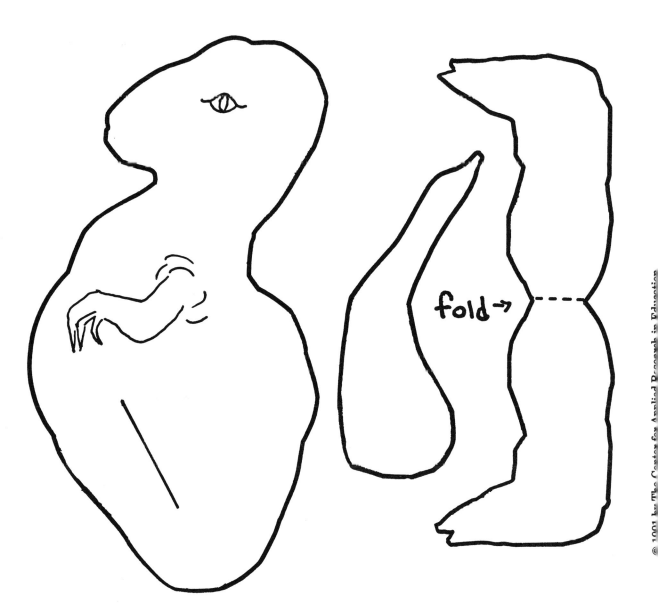

fold →

Stegosaurus

STEGOSAURUS

Duckbill Dinosaur

Number Soup

P Is for Panda

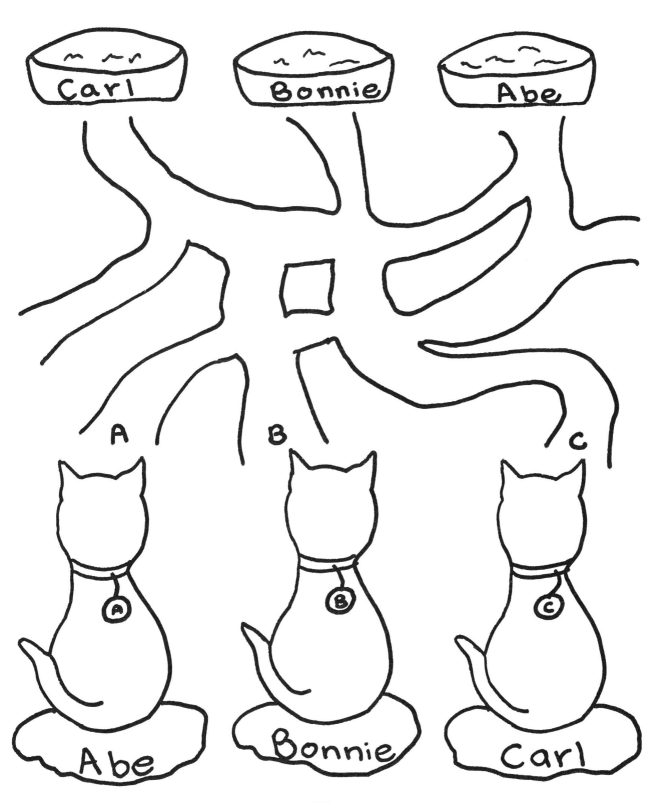

Ice Cream Cones
For Me
For My Friend

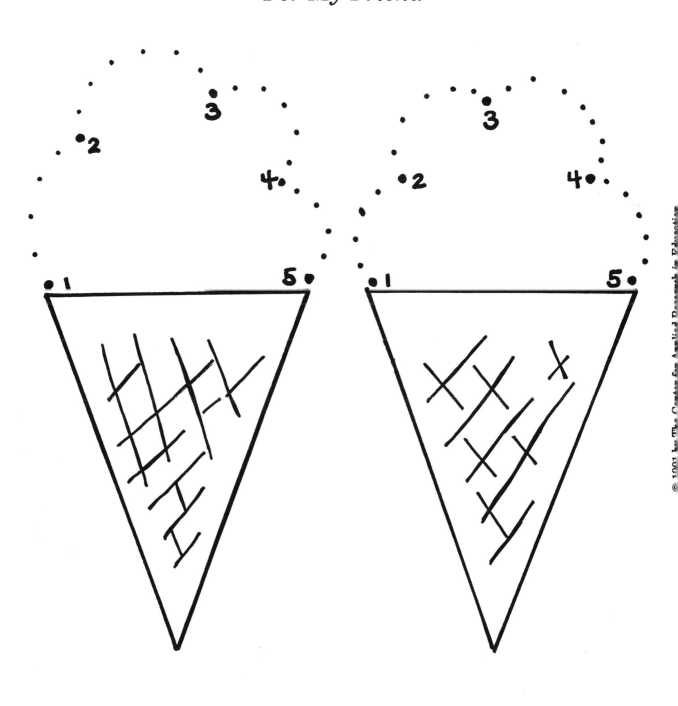

Mobile

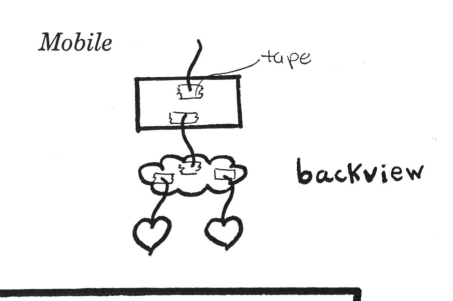

tape

backview

Dr. King

A Dream

Peace

Equality

Snowflakes

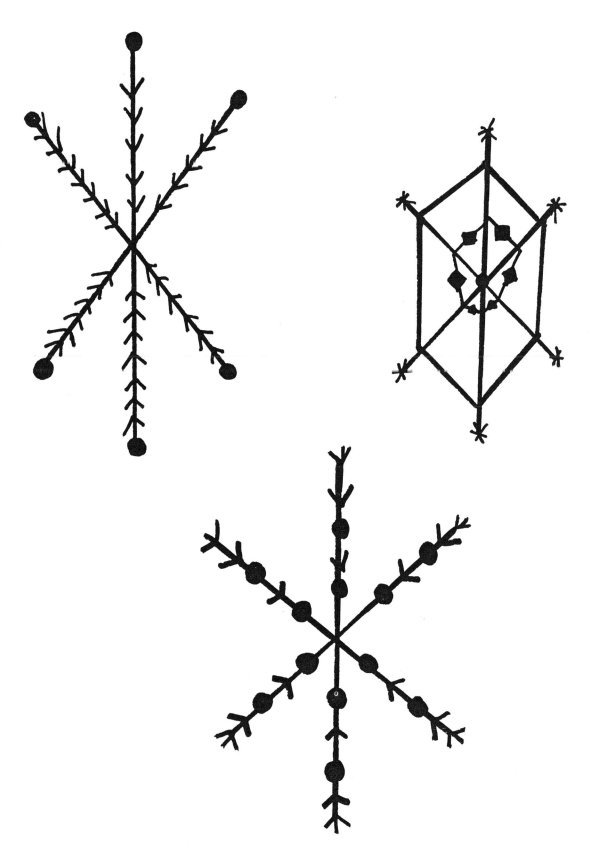

Snowballs

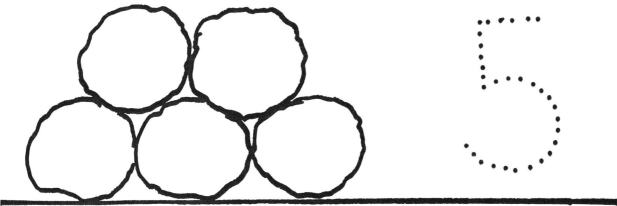

Ice House

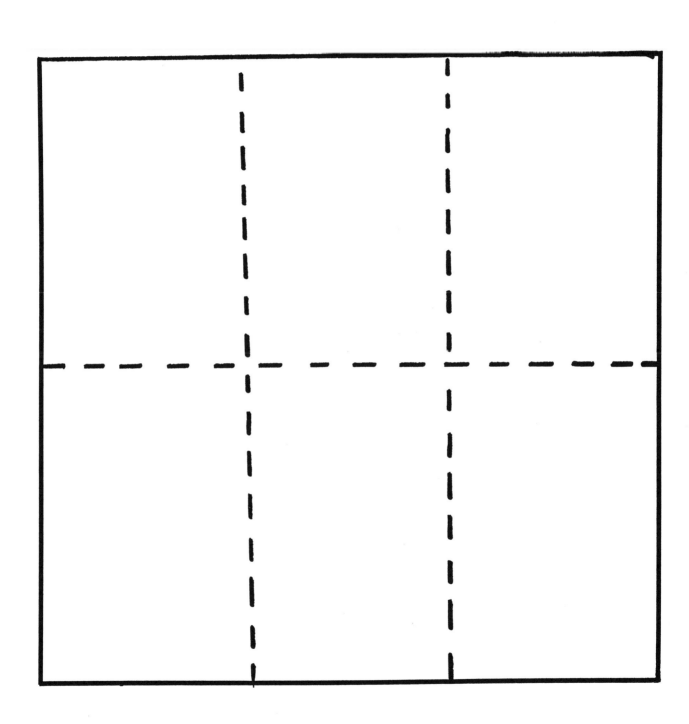

January Mittens

Make a Snowman

Mitten Match

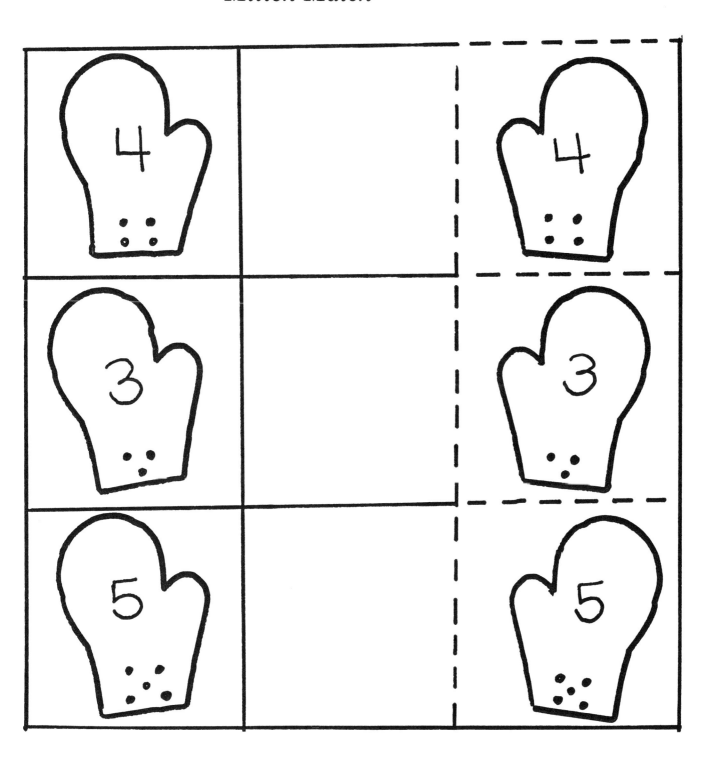

February—Love to All!

A month for all—Woody, Abe, George, and Cupid—to celebrate. Coloring, cutting, and counting will keep the children busy during this short but eventful month. We will discuss the famous presidents, the love in our hearts, and that unpredictable groundhog.

Beginnings

FEBRUARY

Dear Parents:

February is going to be a busy month in preschool!

We'll start the month by looking to see if our furry, underground friend sees his shadow. We'll discuss and experiment with the concept of shadows.

Love will be in the air as we discuss how we can show our love to those who love us through caring and sharing. The children will be making Valentines to bring home to give to the special people in their lives.

Our two famous presidents will inspire our math readiness work.

Join in our month of celebrations by discussing with your child your family traditions and relationships, as well as what it means to be president!

♡ from Preschool,

_____

Share the following wonderful stories with your children.

Secret Valentine by Laura Damon (Troll Associates)

Molly the mouse receives a cheese heart from a secret admirer. She visits all her friends, and asks if they are her secret friend. Finally, she finds Wally—and they share Valentine's Day together happily.

This is a good book to spark a conversation about having friends and feeling "special."

The Old Man and the Afternoon Cat by Michaela Muntean (Parents Magazine Press)

This is a very cute story about how love changes a grouchy old man into a "sweetheart." The book includes two songs, "I Hate Birthdays" and "I Like Birthdays," that the children are sure to enjoy.

Joey by Jack Kent (Prentice Hall)

Joey, a young kangaroo, is bored and lonely in his mother's pouch. However, madcap fun begins when Joey's friends arrive. The author pokes gentle humor at relations between parents and children.

It's My Birthday! by Shigeo Watanabe (Philomel Books)

This is a story of Bear's very special fourth birthday celebration. The photos in an album from Grandma and Grandpa show the warmth and gentle humor of growing up with family and friends.

Invite the children to talk about their family celebrations.

Ten, Nine, Eight by Molly Bang (Greenwillow Books)

This book, about a bedtime countdown, makes going to sleep a warm and secure event. Love and caring abound!

Since many preschoolers experience "going-to-bed jitters," this book sets the stage for the children to air their own feelings.

Arthur's Valentine by Marc Brown (Little, Brown & Co.)

Arthur tries to discover his secret admirer. Valentine notes, jokes, and kidding make for a funny story and a good opener for discussions about feelings.

What's Missing? by Niki Yektai (Clarion Books)

This concept book is filled with funny surprises. Pre-K students enthusiastically provide the answers to each page's question, "What's missing?"

This book is a good introduction to the game "What's Missing?" and the "What's Missing?" readiness sheet found later in this section.

_____ READINESS ACTIVITIES FOR FEBRUARY _____

Love Is Sharing

Make a copy of the "Love Is Sharing" worksheet for each student. Say, "Make believe all the candy in the bag is yours. Three of your friends put out their hands and ask for a piece. Share your candy. Color the candy, cut it out, and glue the correct piece each friend wants on that friend's hand. How many pieces of candy do you have left?"

Share some real candy with the children in the class.

Have a Heart

Make a copy of the "Have a Heart" worksheet for each child. Help with the written directions. Then say, "How many 'h's are on this worksheet? Put a circle around every large and small 'h.'"

Take a walk around the school with the children and discover some of the places that make your school such a special place. You'll find the secretary's office, cafeteria, supply closet, and so on.

A Rosey Rose

Known as the flower of love, the rose is one of the most familiar flowers in the world. It is England's national flower.

Make a copy of "A Rosey Rose" worksheet for each child. Say, "Color this rose valentine carefully. Then cut it out and give it to someone you love."

My Heart's Aflutter

Make a copy of the "My Heart's Aflutter" worksheet for each student. Say, "Make a valentine for someone you love. Go over the words on the hearts with a red marker, then cut out the hearts. Color the three birds. Fold the hearts in half. Put glue on the blank half of the hearts and put them on the birds as shown by the dotted lines."

I Give You My Heart

Make a copy of the "I Give You My Heart" worksheet for each student. Say, "Make this valentine look like you. Look in a mirror. What color is your hair? Your eyes? What colors are the clothes you're wearing? Cut out the valentine on the heavy black lines. Fold the arm as indicated. Write 'I give you . . .' on the blank side of the heart."

Three Hearts

Have the children fold a piece of white construction paper in thirds and draw a heart as shown. Help them to cut on the lines. Open the paper and ask them to write "I" on the first heart, color the middle heart red, and write "YOU" on the third heart. Refold the paper and let the children give their valentine to someone they love.

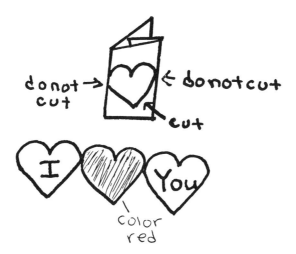

Heart Doily

Fold a piece of pink construction paper in half and draw half a heart on it. Cut out the heart. While the heart is still folded in half, help the children cut out triangle and half-circle shapes from the heart's edges. Then open the heart and glue it onto red construction paper.

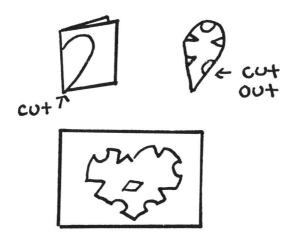

Miss (or Mr.) Heart

Have the children cut out a heart from construction paper. Draw eyes, nose, and a smile on the heart. Help the children to accordion-pleat four long strips of construction paper. Glue them on the heart for legs and arms. The students can add hair with tissue paper strips or yarn.

Sponge-Painted Heart

Draw a heart on construction paper. Put a small amount of red and white tempera paint in a cup or small bowl; do not mix them together. Have the children dip a small piece of sponge into the paint and dab it up and down around the edge of the heart. The children should repeat this until they get to the center of the heart. By the time they reach the center of the heart, the red and white paint will have mixed together to make pink.

Heart Flower

From half a sheet of construction paper, cut out a heart. Draw a smiling face on the heart. Attach it to two construction paper leaves with an accordion-pleated green construction paper strip. On one leaf write, "My Love"; on the other leaf, write "Grows and Grows."

Sew a Heart

Cut a large heart from red construction paper. With a hole puncher, make holes around the edge of the heart. Tie a piece of yarn in one hole and let the children pull the yarn in and out of the holes. (Put a piece of cellophane tape on the end of the yarn to make it stiff.)

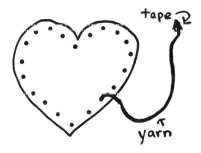

George's Cherry Trees

Make a copy of the "George's Cherry Trees" worksheet for each child. Say, "George Washington, our first president, was very good in mathematics. Can you count as well as President Washington? How many cherries are on each tree? Go over the numeral in each box."

When the children have completed the worksheet, let them color all the trees and cherries. Then make some "cherries" out of clay. Put a clay cherry on top of each cherry on the worksheet. Have the children count them again.

The Height of Abraham Lincoln

Cut out a top hat from black construction paper. Then say, "Abraham Lincoln was our 16th—and, so far, the tallest—president. He was 6 feet 4 inches tall! Let's measure President Lincoln's height on the wall and mark it with this top hat."

Have the children stand by the wall and mark their heights with top hats, too.

A Lincoln Medal

Cut a circle out of cardboard. With a pencil, divide it into six segments. Color the segments alternately with red and blue. Say to the children, "President Lincoln was such a special president that the government stamps his face on billions of pennies every year."

Show a penny to the children. Then glue it in the center of the circle (this completes the medal), and use string so that the medal can be worn. Now help each child make his or her own medal in the same way, so that the children can wear them to celebrate Lincoln's birthday.

Show the children three piles of pennies, of various heights. Which pile has the most pennies? Which has the least? Ask the children to count the pennies in each pile. Can they make the piles the same height?

Have the children close their eyes and put out their hands. Put a different number of pennies in each hand. Can they tell which hand feels heavier?

Put five pennies in one hand. Can the children feel and count the pennies with their eyes closed?

Let's Make Es

Give each child a pile of 3″ × ½″ rectangles, a pile of 2″ × ½″ rectangles, and a piece of construction paper. Ask the children to make as many Es as they can. Remind them to put the long rectangle straight up and down first. Then glue the Es on the paper.

Make some sandpaper Es for tactile reinforcement of the E shape. With a pencil, make a large E on construction paper, and go over it with glue. Have each child sprinkle sand on their E. Shake off the excess sand. Let it dry. Have the children "feel" the E.

E Wants to Eat

Make a copy of the "E Wants to Eat" worksheet for each child. Say, "The word EATING starts with an E. This E wants to EAT—it's very hungry! Draw a line from the E to those things that are good to eat. Then color all the food that the E is going to eat. Go over the E with your marker or crayon."

Ask the children what they like to eat. Have them look through supermarket flyers or magazines and ask them to cut out pictures of things they like to eat. Glue the pictures onto construction paper.

Woody

Make a copy of the "Woody" worksheet for each child. Say, "As legend tells us, on February 2, Groundhog Day, Woody comes out of his burrow, where he has hibernated for the winter, to see if it is Spring yet. If he sees his shadow, we'll have six more weeks of Winter. If not, Spring's just around the corner.

"Color Woody and his burrow brown. Cut them out. Tape the edges of the burrow together. Glue Woody onto a craft stick and put him in his burrow. Hold the burrow in one hand, and Woody's stick in the other. You can now make Woody come up and down out of his burrow."

Woody's Shadow

Turn off the lights in the room and shine a flashlight on Woody. (Tell the children to pretend that the flashlight is the sun.) Do they see Woody's shadow? If it's sunny when the children take Woody home, ask them to hold Woody near the sidewalk and look for his shadow.

On a sunny day, take the children outside and have them look for their shadows. Let the children trace each other's shadow with chalk.

Rectangle Bridges

With rectangle wooden blocks, have the children build bridges to match yours.

Ask, "How many rectangles did it take to build this bridge? Which bridge would be best for a big truck to go under? Which bridge is the tallest? The shortest?"

Over and Under the Bridge

Give each child a small toy car. Ask the children to put the car UNDER the bridge, OVER the bridge, NEXT TO the bridge, BEHIND the bridge, and IN FRONT OF the bridge.

Shadow Tag

If it's sunny outside, show the children how to play Shadow Tag: Each child touches the shadow of another child with his or her foot and then runs away so that no one else can catch his or her shadow.

What's Missing?

Make a copy of the "What's Missing?" worksheet for each child. Say, "Look at the train. What is it missing? Draw a line towards its missing part. Do the same thing with the other pictures."

Read the book *What's Missing?* (see "February Storytime").

——————— MUSIC AND MOVEMENT ———————

We Care

Here's a play for seven children. You can easily add or subtract lines if necessary.

Child 1: We show we care. . . .
Child 2: When we don't step on flowers in the garden (*holds up flowers*)
Child 1: We show we care. . . .
Child 3: When we help someone do a puzzle (*holds up a puzzle*)
Child 1: We show we care. . . .
Child 4: When we say "Come let's play" (*wave hand to come*)
Child 1: We show we care. . . .
Child 5: When we share our toys (*holds out toy*)
Child 1: We show we care. . . .
Child 6: When we take care of ourselves (*hugs self*)
Child 1: We show we care. . . .
Child 7: When we're 'real' nice to each other.
          (*All children put hands on each others' shoulders*)
ALL: Happy Valentine's Day!

Shadows

> Short or tall (*squat, stand tall*)
> Big or small (*reach way out, in close*)
> Shadows dance
> Up on the wall. (*walk fingers up a wall*)
> Shadows thin (*put up index finger*)
> Shadows round (*form circle with thumb and index fingers*)
> Shadows creeping
> On the ground. (*walk fingers on the floor*)

Light and Shadows

Shine the light from a movie or slide projector against a wall in a darkened room. Have the children do a shadow dance. It's also fun to teach the children how to make animal shadows using their hands and fingers.

_____ SONGS, POEMS, AND FINGERPLAYS _____

Woody's Ditty

Have the children look in a newspaper for a picture of a real groundhog. Ask them, "Why is this groundhog called 'Woody'?" (He's a woodchuck.) Then teach them the following ditty:

> How much wood
> Would a woodchuck chuck
> If a woodchuck
> Could chuck wood?

_____ FROM BUTTON'S COUNTRY KITCHEN _____

George's Miniature Cheese Cakes

2 8–ounce packages cream cheese
2 eggs
¾ cup sugar
1 T. lemon juice

1 tsp. vanilla
1 can of cherry pie filling
vanilla wafers
midget-sized foil baking cups

Soften the cream cheese at room temperature. Add the sugar, eggs, lemon juice, and vanilla. Use the mixer at high speed for about 5 minutes. Set up the foil baking cups on a cookie sheet and set 1 wafer in each cup. Spoon the cheese mixture ¾ of the way into each cup. Bake at 350° for 8–10 minutes. Let cool on rack and then spoon 1 tsp. of cherry filling on each. Refrigerate until ready to use.

Marzipan Candy Hearts

1 cup almond paste   ¼ tsp. salt
1 egg white   2 cups confectioners' sugar

Beat the egg white and mix with the almond paste. Add the salt and enough sugar to make the mixture stiff enough to handle. Knead 10 to 15 minutes and place in a covered glass dish. After about 24 hours, the marzipan is ready to mold. Color with red food coloring, if desired, and mold into small hearts.

————————— VIDEOS FOR FEBRUARY —————————

The Mother Goose Treasury (J2 Communications, 1987)

The "Puppetronics" used in this video make these timeless Mother Goose songs, rhymes, and stories come alive. Volumes I, II, III, and IV are all great! Approximate running time: 30 minutes each.

Polly's Pet (Golden Book Video, Western Publishing, 1985)

This is a nice winter/Valentine story. Tired of the insults heaped upon him by his well-meaning masters, Polly's Pet runs away from home. Much to his surprise, he finds that fun isn't fun unless it's shared, and that home is really where the heart is. This 30-minute tape also includes "The Tale of Peter Rabbit" and "The Little Red Hen."

————————— WORKSHEETS FOR FEBRUARY —————————

The following worksheets are referred to in this month's readiness activities.

Love Is Sharing

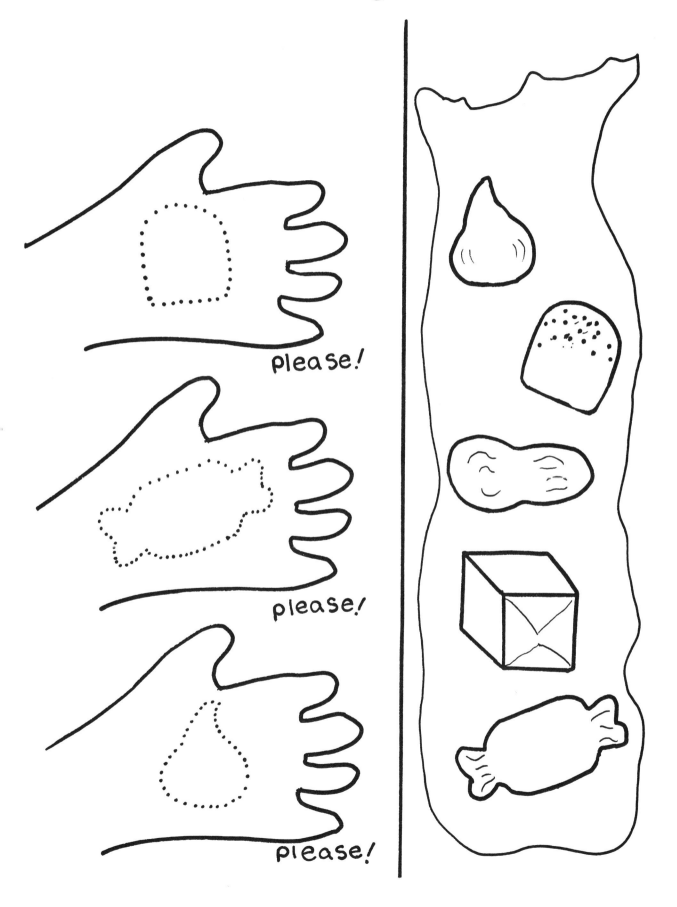

please!

please!

please!

Have a Heart

How can Harriet find Harvey? Have a heart and help her find him. Draw a line to show how Harriet should travel.

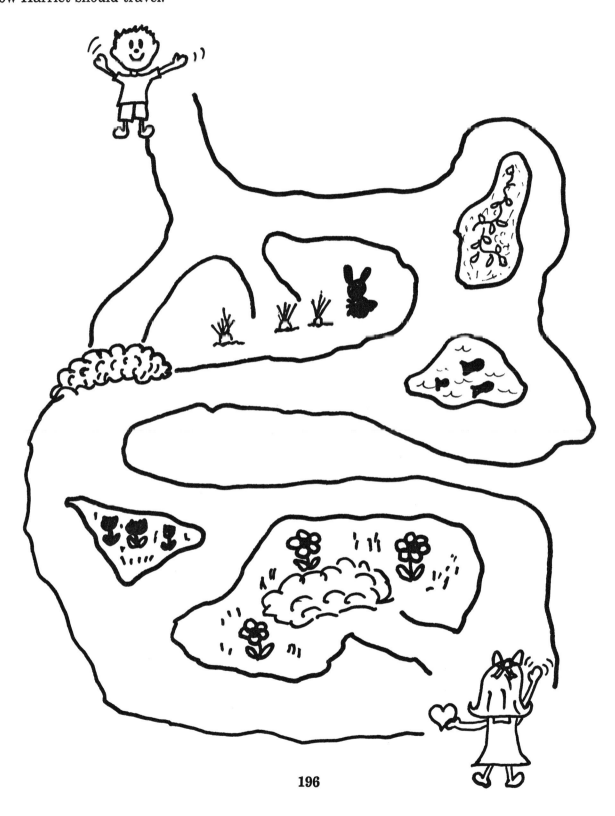

196

A Rosey Rose

My Heart's Aflutter

I Give You My Heart

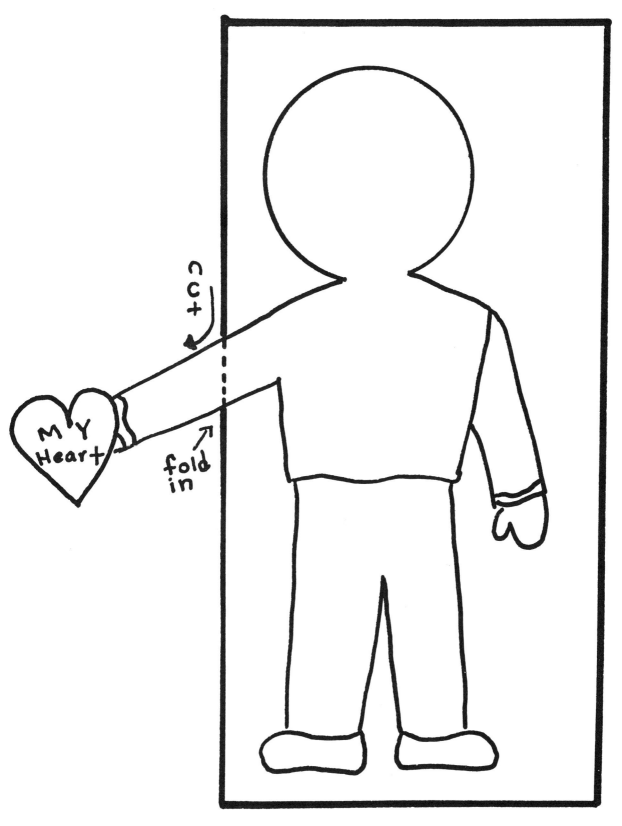

cut

fold
in

MY
Heart

George's Cherry Trees

E Wants to Eat

Woody

202

What's Missing?

March Is Breezing By

This breezy month is filled with lots of green fun and fantasy. Shaughnessy Shawn the Leprechaun has a delightful mix of activites to suit everyone's fancy!

Beginnings

MARCH

Dear Parents:

Our preschool year is certainly breezing by! March, our breezy month, will bring a rustle of activities that are aimed at providing the children with skill builders that are sure to please.

Shaughnessy Shawn the Leprechaun wants us all to celebrate his special day, so the children will be immersed in shamrocks, shillelaghs, shenanigans, and potatoes!

"Top o' the mornin'" from preschool.

Sincerely,

_____

This month's books are full of March delights. Share these with your children.

The Wind Blew by PAT HUTCHINS (Macmillan Publishing)

This nicely illustrated book begins with "The wind blew." It's about the various possessions the wind takes up in the air.

This book is good to read at the start of your windy projects. Other wind books are: *Curious George Flies a Kite* by Margaret Rey (Houghton Mifflin), *Jonathan Plays With the Wind* by Kathryn Galleant (Coward-McCann), *The Red Balloon* by Albert Lamorisse (Doubleday), *Gilberto and the Wind* by Marie Hall Ets (Viking Press), and *A Letter for Amy* by Ezra Jack Keats (Harper & Row).

Jeremy Bean's St. Patrick's Day by ALICE SCHERTLE (Lothrop, Lee and Shepard Books)

Jeremy Bean plans a "green" St. Patrick's Day party for his class. Things don't go too well until Jeremy gets a helping hand from a surprising new friend.

This is a good story to read before planning your class party.

St. Patrick's Day in the Morning by ERIC BUNTING (Houghton Mifflin)

Jamie Donovan is the only family member who is too small to walk in the St. Patrick's Day Parade. In the spirit of the day, he and his dog create their own parade. The book is an excellent illustration of Ireland's rugged countryside.

Create a St. Patrick's Parade of your own. Safety-pin paper shamrocks on all the children and use your rhythm instruments to march to an Irish tune.

Green Eyes by A. BIRNBAUM (Golden Press)

Green Eyes, a tiny white kitten, experiences each season's delights as he explores his home on the farm. This is a good book for the discussion of seasonal changes in our environment.

Now Can We Go? by ANN JONAS (Greenwillow Books)

The author shows—through beautiful illustrations and simple wording—the feelings of a young child who packs for a trip away from home. Youngsters are sure to relate to the feelings expressed in this story.

Wake Up, Bear by LYNLEY DODD (Gareth Stevens Publishing)

Despite all their efforts, none of the forest animals can get Bear to wake up from his winter sleep. A buzzing bee does the trick and wakes up the honey-hungry bear!

Grizzly Bear by LYNNE CHERRY (E. P. Dutton & Co.)

This is a short but beautifully illustrated story about a grizzly bear family waking up after their long winter nap.

READINESS ACTIVITIES FOR MARCH

What Is Green?

Green is the color for St. Patrick's Day. To peak the children's interest in this secondary color, do this color science "magic": Fill a clear glass with water, squeeze a drop of blue food coloring into the water, and mix; then add a drop of yellow food coloring and mix. Presto—green! Let the children experiment themselves.

Have the children think of things that are green: grapes, frogs, leaves, cartoon characters, etc. Give the children old magazines, department store catalogs, and/or supermarket flyers to look through for pictures of green things. Have the children cut out the pictures and make a chart to classify the pictures as "Things You Can Eat" and "Things You Cannot Eat." Invite the children to come one at a time to the chart and put their pictures under the appropriate heading. Use a glue stick to attach the pictures to the chart.

Green Grapes

Make a copy of the "Green Grapes" worksheet for each child. Say, "The grape is a fruit—or more exactly, a berry—that grows in bunches on a vine. It is one of the oldest plants known to man and grows in every country in the world. Look at the worksheet. How many grapes are in each child's hand? Count the grapes and go over the numeral. Then color all the grapes green."

Bring in a bunch of green grapes. Ask each child to count and pick off two grapes, three grapes, and so on.

Give the children a skin-tone crayon and white paper. Have them trace their hand onto the paper. Ask, "How many grapes do you want to eat?" Have the children use green crayons to draw the grapes on their paper hand.

G Is for Grape

Make a copy of the "G Is for Grape" worksheet for each child. Say, "A lot of Gs are hiding in the grapes. With a marker or crayon, go over each G you can find. Then color all the grapes that do *not* have a G in them."

Green Snakes

Give each child some yellow and some blue clay, then have them squeeze the two colors together. As they knead, the clay will turn green. Show the children how to take small pieces of clay and roll them on the table with the palm of the hand to form "snakes." Ask the children to see how many snakes can be made with their ball of clay.

Community Helper—Dentist

Ask your local dentist to lend you a model of a set of teeth. Or better yet, ask the dentist to come in to talk to the children about good dental health. (Children love it if you use the set of teeth to talk about good dental hygiene.)

Demonstrate brushing the teeth, and emphasize the importance of reaching to the back. Dentists, or your local dental society, usually have pamphlets on brushing. Let the children take turns "brushing" the set of teeth. Discuss foods that are good for you and your teeth.

Make a copy of the "Finish the Toothbrushes" worksheet for each child. Say, "Color each toothbrush a different color. Make nice straight bristles on each of them with your pencil."

Shaughnessy Shawn's Hat

Make a copy of the "Shaughnessy Shawn's Hat" worksheet for each child. Say, "Color this leprechaun's hat green. Staple the band on the hat. Measure it around your head and staple it closed." (Extend the band if necessary to fit around the child's head.)

Have the children wear their hats as they sing and dance like Shaughnessy Shawn the leprechaun. (See "Songs, Poems, and Fingerplays" for Shaughnessy's song.)

Grow Shamrocks

Purchase clover seeds in the summer. Have the children plant the seeds a few weeks before St. Patrick's Day in containers in the classroom. Observe the growth process. If the clover is mixed, have the children discriminate between 3– and 4– leaf clovers.

Green Carnation Greetings

Make a copy of the "Green Carnation Greetings" worksheet for each child. Say, "Carnations are usually seen in the colors red, white, and pink. But in March, people wear a lot of green carnations. These carnations don't grow that way. They are white carnations that are put in water with green dye. The flower sucks the green coloring up through its stem." Then try this experiment in your classroom.

Continue by saying, "Here are some paper carnations that you can color green with your crayon. Cut them out and give them to your family members. Remember to say 'Happy St. Patrick's Day!' "

Sponge-Painted Shamrock

Put a small amount of blue and yellow paints in a cup or bowl. With a coffee stirrer, have the children mix these two primary colors to get the secondary color of green. Show them that you can make the green darker by adding more blue, or lighter by adding more yellow. Then make a copy of the "Sponge-Painted Shamrock" worksheet for each child. Say, "Dip a small piece of sponge in the paint and slide it around on the outline of this shamrock. Dip and slide the middle of your shamrock until it is all colored in."

Shamrock Hunt

Make a copy of the "Shamrock Hunt" worksheet for each child. Say, "A shamrock is a plant that has three leaves. Hiding in this field of shamrocks, however, are some four-leaf clovers! Color all the three-leaf shamrocks green. Make sure you count the number of leaves before you start to color."

The Versatile Potato

Potatoes are a very popular vegetable. They are a nourishing and healthful food that contains a large amount of starch. They are cooked many different ways. Potatoes are associated with Ireland because in the 19th century the Irish people were very dependent on potatoes as their staple food.

Bring in a bag of potatoes and let the children feel and count them. Draw or show the children a picture of how potatoes grow underground.

Have the children pick out the smallest, the largest, and the fattest potato, etc. Weigh the potatoes on a scale. Have the children take turns closing their eyes and let them try to feel which of two potatoes is heavier.

Use the largest potato to play "Hot Potato"—to an Irish tune, of course!

Declare a Potato Week. Have each child bring in a potato each day. (Be sure to have potatoes on hand in case some children forget or are unable to bring in a potato.) Make different potato recipes, being sure to follow all safety rules. Here are some suggested recipes:

Mashed Potatoes

Peel potatoes and cut in halves or thirds. Boil till soft. Mash. Add milk, butter, and salt to taste.

Baked Potatoes

Wash and prick potatoes with a fork. Bake potatoes in a 350° oven for 45 minutes to 1 hour or until they feel soft when pricked with a fork. Serve with butter, margarine, or sour cream.

Boiled Potato Balls or Cubes

1 pound of potatoes
1 teaspoon salt
3 tablespoons melted butter or margarine

Peel the potatoes and cut them into balls with vegetable or melon scoop or cut into cubes. Drop the potatoes into boiling water and boil for 15 minutes or until tender. Pour melted butter or margarine over them. Sprinkle lightly with salt.

French Fried Potatoes

Peel potatoes. Slice strips 2 inches long and ½ inch thick. Fry in oil until golden brown. Drain on paper towels.

Hashed Browned Potatoes

Heat 2 tablespoons of oil in a frying pan. Add 2 cups finely chopped cold boiled potatoes, 1 tablespoon chopped parsley, ½ teaspoon salt, and a few grains of pepper. Mix thoroughly, then allow the potatoes to brown on the underside. Fold over like an omelet.

Potatoes Au Gratin

Grease a baking dish. Arrange slices of cold boiled potatoes on the bottom. Sprinkle with grated cheese, salt, and pepper. Dot with butter. Repeat this process until all ingredients are used. Add enough milk to almost cover top layer. Bake in 400° oven 20–25 minutes.

Scalloped Potatoes

Follow recipe for potatoes au gratin, eliminating cheese and sprinkling a little flour on each layer.

Potato Cakes

Mold cold mashed potatoes into patties. Dredge with flour. Fry in a little shortening, turning once to brown both sides.

Potato Pancakes

3 medium-sized raw potatoes	1 egg
1 tablespoon flour	1 teaspoon salt
1 tablespoon onion	

Grate potatoes and onions. Add other ingredients. Stir well. Cook in hot oil until brown. Drop by spoonfuls into frying pan.

Potato Salad

1 cup mayonnaise	1 tablespoon sugar
2 tablespoons vinegar	¼ teaspoon pepper
1½ teaspoon salt	4 cups cooked, cubed, peeled potatoes
2 hard cooked eggs, chopped (optional)	(5–6 medium potatoes)

Combine all ingredients except potatoes and eggs. Mix in potatoes and eggs. Cover and chill.

Mr. or Mrs. Potato

Make a copy of the "Mr. or Mrs. Potato" worksheet for each child. Say, "With your markers, give your potato eyes, a nose, and a mouth. Color the potato lightly with your brown crayon. Color the hat and the shamrock. Cut out all the pieces. Glue the potato on a piece of construction paper. Glue the hat onto the potato's head and the shamrock under its chin.

Shaughnessy Shawn Bag Puppet

Make a copy of the "Shaughnessy Shawn Bag Puppet" worksheet for each child. Say, "Color these pieces of Shaughnessy. Cut them out. Then glue them to a lunch bag as shown." Have the children's puppets sing Shaughnessy's song that's given in "Music and Movement."

Shaughnessy's Shillelagh

A shillelagh is an Irish walking stick carved out of wood from a forest in Ireland called Shillelagh.

Make a copy of the "Shaughnessy's Shillelagh" worksheet for each child. Say, "Make your shillelagh look like it was carved by coloring the carving marks with your black crayon. Color the rest of the shillelagh with brown crayon. Count all the carving marks, then cut out the three pieces of the shillelagh. Tape them together or glue them onto a piece of green construction paper."

Pots of Gold

Make a copy of the "Pots of Gold" worksheet for each child. Say, "Leprechauns love gold! Here are some pots of gold for you. Collect 21 pennies, and pile the correct number of pennies on each pot of gold. Then remove the pennies, go over all the numerals with your green crayon, and then lightly color the pots black."

Fun With Air and Wind

March is a good month to discuss and demonstrate the uses and effects of air and wind. You can begin by having the children inhale air through their noses and exhale through their mouths. Then reverse the activity to show the children how their mouths and noses are connected. Have them feel the exhalation by putting their hands near their noses and mouths. Discuss how you can feel air but not see it. Have the children blow cotton balls, feathers, paper balls, and so on, to see the effect of their exhaling. Give them small balloons to blow up. (If some children have difficulty with this, even just their attempts to blow into the balloon will show them how the balloon can "trap" their air.) Release an inflated balloon to demonstrate the concept of escaping air. Have the children pretend to be balloons—ask them to stand tall, inhale, hold their breath for a moment, and then slowly exhale and "float" to the floor.

On a windy day, go outside and give each child a streamer. They will experience the feel of the wind and see how it moves the streamers. Have them twirl and jump. Organize a streamer parade. Count out a marching beat for the children with rhythm sticks, then have the children hold their streamers high in the wind and march behind you around the playground.

Another way to demonstrate how air feels is to have the children hold the edges of an old sheet or parachute, and watch the wind pick it up and down.

Making a Windsock

1. Cut a 9″ × 12″ piece of construction paper in half the long way.

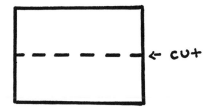

2. Give each child half a sheet of paper and have them decorate it.

3. Fold the paper in half the long way with the decorations on the outside. Glue strips of crepe paper, colored tissue paper, or streamers inside the fold.

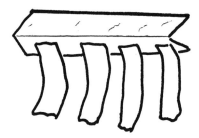

4. Form the paper into a cylinder and staple it closed. Punch a hole in each side and string with yarn.

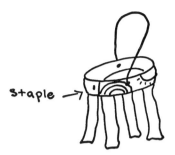

5. Hold the middle of the string and run on the playground.

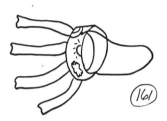

Mary's Lamb

Make a copy of the "Mary's Lamb" worksheet for each child. Say, "The weather at the end of March is supposed to be soft and gentle like a lamb. Color your lamb's face, tail, and legs, then take a cotton ball and pull it apart. Put glue on the lamb and stick the cotton on." The children can sing and act out "Mary Had a Little Lamb."

The March Wind

Make a copy of "The March Wind" worksheet for each child. Say, "The March wind has blown the children's hats off their heads. Fortunately, they have their names on their hats. Color the hats and cut them out. Match their names and glue each hat on its owner's head."

A March Kite

Make a copy of "A March Kite" worksheet for each child. Say, "March is a windy month—a good month to fly a kite! Go over the word MARCH. Then draw and color some flowers on the kite. We hope to see some peeking their heads up at the end of the month. Cut out the kite. Tape or tie a 12–inch piece of string to the top of the kite. Then color the bows for the kite's tail. Cut them apart where shown and tape them to another 12–inch piece of string. Tape this tail to the bottom of the kite." Then bring the children outside on a windy day to see if their kites will fly.

————————— MUSIC AND MOVEMENT —————————

Shaughnessy's Song

> I'm Shaughnessy Shawn, the Leprechaun,
> I dance all day and I sing this song.
> My pot of gold you'll never find,
> Unless, of course, you catch me!

Shaughnessy's Game

Have all the children sit in a circle. One child is picked as "Shaughnessy." This child walks around the outside circle of children and sings Shaughnessy's song. After Shaughnessy says "Unless, of course, you catch me," Shaughnessy touches one of the children's shoulders. This child gets up and tries to catch Shaughnessy, who runs around the circle and tries to get back to the vacant spot. If caught, Shaughnessy sits in the center of the circle (the pot of gold). Proceed until all the children have a chance to play Shaughnessy.

The March Wind

> The March Wind is a silly clown
> He blows the leaves up (*stretch up arms, stand tippy-toed*)
> He blows the leaves down (*sit on the floor*)
> He blows the leaves all around (*stand and turn around*)
> He blows them to the left (*move to the left*)
> He blows them to the right (*move to the right*)
> And now he's going to blow my kite. (*make believe you're holding a kite*)

————————— SONGS, POEMS, AND FINGERPLAYS —————————

Mary Had a Little Lamb

Have one child be "Mary" to lead the class in a walk either around your room, or outside. All the other class members should follow Mary "wherever she goes." You might have the children carry the lambs they make in the project "Mary's Lamb."

> Mary had a little lamb,
> Little lamb, little lamb.
> Mary had a little lamb
> With fleece as white as snow.

Everywhere that Mary went,
Mary went, Mary went
Everywhere that Mary went
That lamb was sure to go.

He followed her to school one day,
School one day, school one day.
He followed her to school one day
Which was against the rules.

It made the children laugh and play,
Laugh and play, laugh and play.
It made the children laugh and play
To see a lamb at school.

Baa-Baa Black Sheep

Baa-Baa black sheep
Have you any wool?
Yes sir, yes sir,
Three bags full.
One for my master,
One for my dame,
And one for the little boy
Who lives down the lane.

Harrigan

H, A, double R, I, GAN
Spells HARRIGAN.
Proud of all the Irish blood that's in me.
Devil a man would say a word agin me.
H, A, double R, I, GAN you see . . .
'Tis a name that a shame
Never has been connected with
HARRIGAN . . . THAT'S ME!

_____ FROM BUTTON'S COUNTRY KITCHEN _____

Green Finger Gelatin

An interesting variation of the standard gelatin recipe will produce a very stiff kind of gelatin that can be eaten with the fingers. You will need:

4 envelopes of unflavored gelatin	1 long-handled wooden spoon
3 3–oz. packages of lime gelatin	1 large bowl
4 cups of boiling water	1 13½″ × 8¼″ × 1½″ baking pan
	(size approximate)

Place both the flavored and unflavored gelatins in a large bowl. Add 4 cups of boiling water, and give each child a turn to carefully stir until the gelatin dissolves. Pour the mixture into a large shallow baking pan and chill in the refrigerator until firm. Use cookie cutters to cut various shamrocks out of the gelatin, or just cut into small squares.

Johnnycake

¾ cup sifted flour	1 teaspoon salt
1½ cups yellow cornmeal	2 well-beaten eggs
1½ teaspoons baking powder	1¼ cups buttermilk
¾ teaspoon baking soda	¼ cup melted butter or margarine

Heat the oven to 400°F. Grease an 8–inch square baking pan. Mix and sift the dry ingredients. Combine the beaten eggs and milk, and add to the dry ingredients. Stir until mixed well. Stir in the melted butter or margarine, and pour into the greased baking pan and bake about 40 minutes.

—————— VIDEOS FOR MARCH ——————

5 Lionni Classics (Random House, 1986)

The enchanting characters in five of Leo Lionni's best-loved children's books—*Frederick, Cornelius, Swimmy, It's Mine,* and *Fish Is Fish*—will delight the children. These fables celebrate the power of imagination, the joy of discovery, and the importance of living together in harmony. Approximate running time: 30 minutes.

—————— WORKSHEETS FOR MARCH ——————

The following worksheets are referred to in this month's readiness activities.

Green Grapes

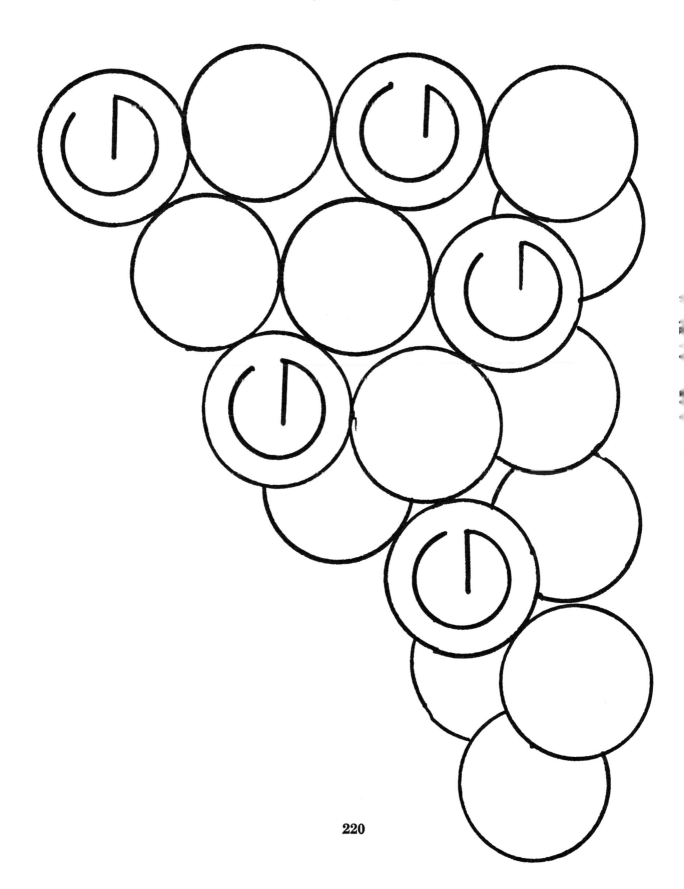

Finish the Toothbrushes

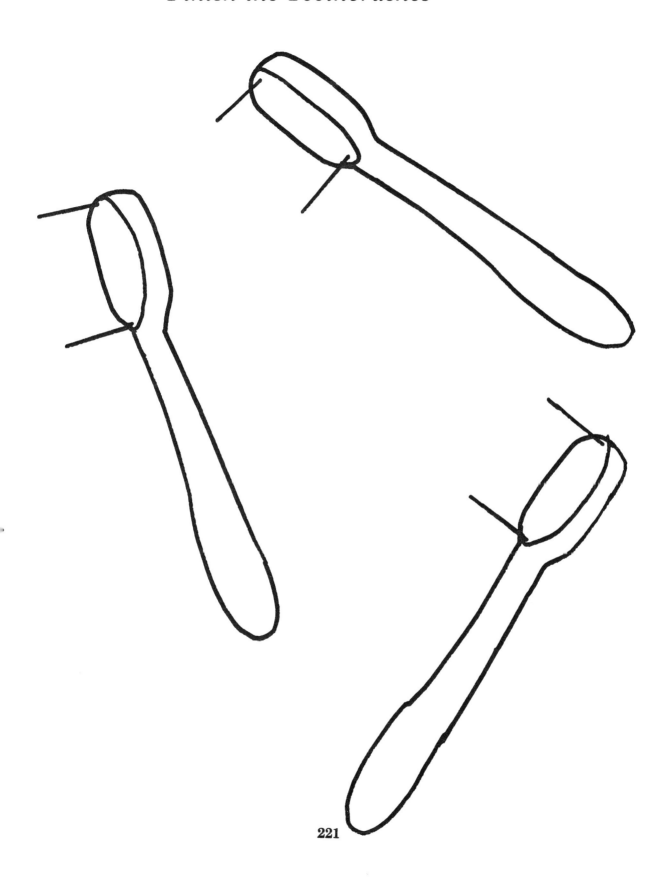

221

Shaughnessy Shawn's Hat

222

Green Carnation Greetings

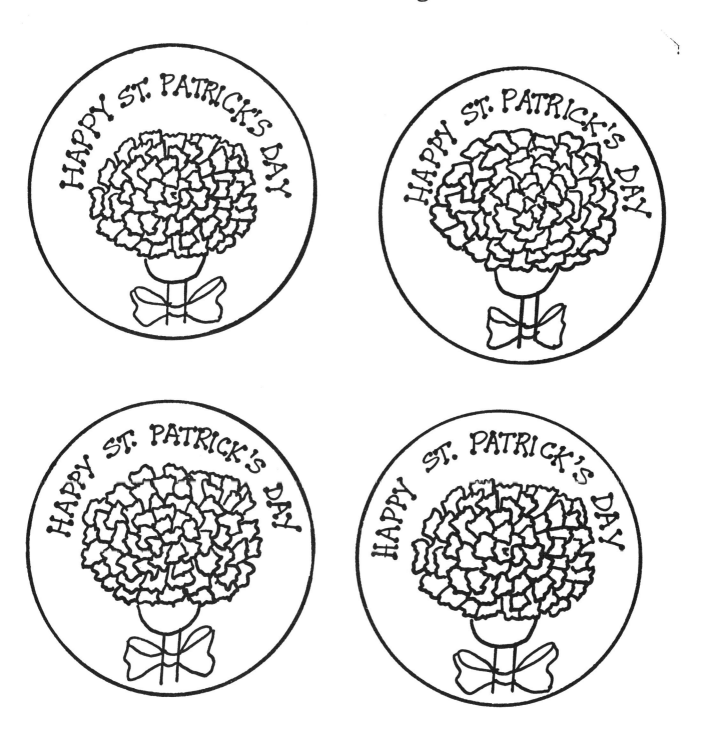

Sponge-Painted Shamrock

Shamrock Hunt

Mr. or Mrs. Potato

Shaughnessy Shawn Bag Puppet

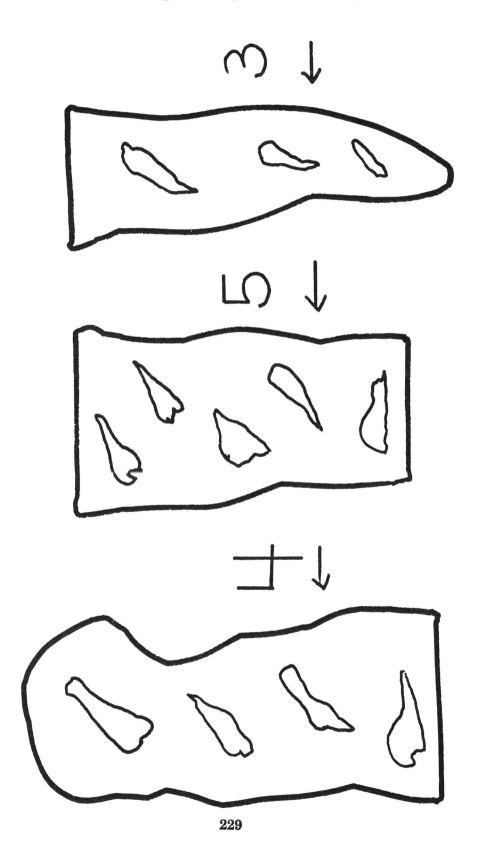

229

Pots of Gold

Mary's Lamb

A March Kite

April — A Shower of Fun

Easter, Passover, flowers, and showers fill this month of April. We will be celebrating Spring and look for nature's new beginning

Beginnings

Dear Parents:

April is here and we're all looking forward to getting outside for playground fun. We'll be looking for signs of spring—listening for the birds, looking for buds on the trees, and enjoying nature's rebirth.

We will be celebrating our spring holidays and honing our early childhood readiness skills.

We wish you a beautiful Spring!

Sincerely,

Introduce your children to the wonders of Spring and the special days this time of year.

Oh, Were They Ever Happy by PETER SPIER (Doubleday & Co.)

This is a funny introduction to the world of color. The Noonan children help out by painting the outside of their home while their parents are away. The result is a very colorful house indeed!

Easter Parade by MARY CHALMERS (Harper & Row)

Animals come from the mountains, the lakes, the woods, and the fields. They fly, swim, hop, and run. They are all flocking to Easter Farm for the annual Grand Animal Parade. This is a touching story of springtime sharing and caring.

The Bunny Who Found Easter by CHARLOTTE ZOLOTOW (Harper & Row)

This is a story of a lonely bunny who goes looking for Easter. His search takes him through each of the seasons. In the spring, he makes a discovery that fills him with joy and shows him the true meaning of Easter.

Look Inside a Tree by GINA INGOGLIA (Grosset and Dunlap)

This is a great book to start your Earth Day or Arbor Day activities. The die-cut holes allow the children to "peek" in to see how a tree grows, how it shelters animals, and how it cleans the air.

The Passover Parrot by EVELYN ZUSMAN (Kar-Ben Copies, Inc.)

This is a delightful story about a busy Jewish family, their Seder, and a young girl's determination to learn the Four Questions in Hebrew. At the end, Hametz, the Passover Parrot, proves to be an inspiration as he practices along with Leba.
Read this story before doing the "Passover Foods" worksheet.

The Great Bunny Race by KATHY FECZKO (Troll Associates)

This is a "you-can-do-it-if-you-try-hard-enough" book. Toby really wants to win the annual bunny race, but feels he's too slow. His friend Darby Duck encourages him to try to do his very best. Toby gives it his all and wins the race. Lesson learned!

Rainbows and Frogs by JOY KIM (Troll Associates)

This is a great book that not only presents colors to children effectively, but points out the special feelings colors can give.

The Very Hungry Caterpillar by ERIC CARLE (Philomel Books)

This strikingly bold and colorful book details one of nature's loveliest marvels—the metamorphosis of the butterfly. The clever die-cut pages show what a caterpillar eats on successive days, before its metamorphosis. It introduces sets of up to 10 objects, names the days of the week, and tells the caterpillar's transformation story.

This is a good story to read with the children before doing the "Miss Caterpillar and Her Cocoon" worksheet.

Other caterpillar books are *Wait for William* by Marjorie Flack (Houghton Mifflin) and *Leo the Late Bloomer* by Robert Kraus (Windmill Books).

Easter Parade by EILEEN CURRAN (Troll Associates)

With Nancy the Easter Chick's help, the Easter Bunny makes enough eggs and baskets to make everyone's Easter happy. Then the Easter Bunny realizes that there is nothing left for his hard-working helper. All the animals in town get together to make Nancy's Easter very special.

After reading this book, take out your instruments and have an Easter parade around your school.

READINESS ACTIVITIES FOR APRIL

Passover Foods

Make a copy of the "Passover Foods" worksheet for each child. Say, "Passover is the Jewish festival of freedom. It comes in late March or early April. The feast is celebrated in memory of the time when the Jews escaped from Egypt. Jews celebrate with a special supper called Seder. Special foods are eaten at this meal: bitter herbs (horseradish), charoses (made from apples, raisins, and sweet wine), three matzos (unleavened crackers), roasted shankbone, roasted egg, and karpas (a green vegetable such as parsley). Color the Seder foods on the worksheet. Decorate the border of the Seder plate. Cut out everything and glue the food onto the dish."

Gather the Seder foods that your children would enjoy tasting and celebrate Passover as a class. During the Seder, you might read *The Passover Parrot*. (See "April Storytime.")

Eggs, Eggs, How Many Eggs?

Set up a spring counting table with the following five areas:

1. *How many?* Put a number of plastic eggs in a basket for the children to count. Make a number strip. Have the children count the eggs in the basket and circle the correct numeral.

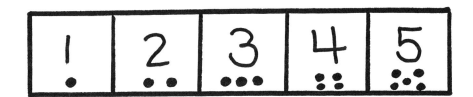

2. *Which Has More?* In two small baskets or plates, place a different number of plastic eggs, plastic bunnies, or plastic flowers. Label your baskets A and B. Call them the "Which has more?" baskets. Have the children count the number of items in each basket, then circle A or B.

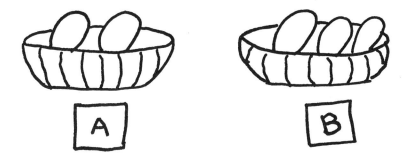

3. *Guess How Many.* Put a small number of jelly beans in a jar. Ask the children to guess how many jelly beans are in the jar, then circle the numeral.

4. *Number Eggs.* Tape paper numbers onto the top of six plastic eggs. Put the eggs in the top half of an egg carton. Have the children put the eggs in order from one to six at the bottom of the carton.

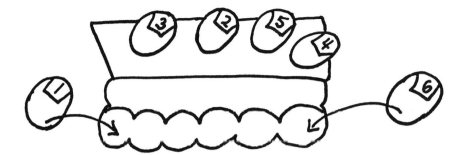

5. *Egg Puzzles.* Cut out five 8″ oaktag eggs. Color each egg a different color. Glue one egg onto the left-hand side of a piece of construction paper. Cut one egg into two pieces and put in an envelope with a 2 marked on the front. Cut another egg into three pieces and mark an envelope with a 3; do the same for 4 and 5. Have the children do the puzzles from 2–5 on the construction paper next to the egg you glue onto the paper.

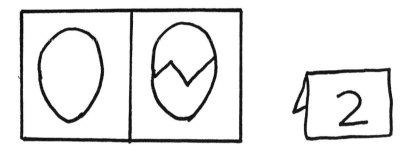

Count and Color

Make a copy of the "Count and Color" worksheet for each child. Say, "How many eggs are in each basket? Look at the numbers on the eggs. Count the eggs, starting with 1. Then color the eggs in bright spring colors and color the baskets. Which basket has more eggs in it? Which basket has fewer eggs in it?"

Wet Chalk Eggs

Eggs are an Easter symbol of a new beginning or rebirth. Here is an art activity using egg shapes. You will need: colored chalks, a small cup half filled with water, and black construction paper for each child. Then say, "On a piece of black construction paper, draw two egg outlines with white or light-colored chalk. Now dip the end of a piece of colored chalk into the water. Color part of the egg. When the chalk stick dries out, dip it back into the water. Use lots of colors to make your eggs look extra special. Let the eggs dry. Aren't the colors beautiful? And they won't smudge like regular chalk drawings."

Make some hard-boiled eggs in class. Use the three primary colors (red, yellow, blue) of food coloring to make secondary colors to dye the eggs.

Cute-as-a-Button Bunny

Make a copy of the "Cute-as-a-Button Bunny" worksheet for each child. Say, "Color Button your favorite bunny color. Cut along the solid lines of the box, then cut out the finger holes. Fold back on the dotted lines. Make a V with your index and middle fingers, and insert them into the finger holes to give Button some ears."

Spring Showers

April is usually a time of many showers. The flower bulbs, trees, bushes, and grass have been waiting all through the winter for these warm showers to come.

Put a plastic cup or bucket outside to collect rain water. Take it in after each April shower and measure the water. Make a chart to show how much water has been collected. (Use the rain water for your indoor plants.) At the end of each week, ask the children, "Which shower gave us the most rain? Which gave us the least?" At the end of the month, ask the questions again.

Our Bucket Collects Rain Water

April 4   April 11   April 18

Discuss each type of shower with the children: "It rained lightly all day long." "It only rained at night while we were sleeping." "The rain came down very hard all morning, then the sun came out." And so on.

Signs of Spring

Take an "It's Spring" walk about your school and look for signs of spring. When you and the children get back to class, sit in a circle and discuss what was seen and heard. Make a "Signs of Spring" book. Which signs of spring were seen? Keep looking for other signs, too. Take the book along when you and the children go out next time.

Raindrops

Make a copy of the "Raindrops" worksheet for each child. Say, "Count the number of raindrops under each umbrella. Go over the numerals. Then color the umbrellas."

Community Helper—Letter Carrier

Most people in the United States have their mail delivered directly to their homes by a letter carrier. The letter carrier collects and sorts the mail at the post office. The carrier then packs his or her bag and begins a route to deliver the mail to you. Benjamin Franklin was the first Postmaster General.

Many post offices give guided tours for children. When you visit a postal facility, bring along a stamped postcard for each child to mail home.

Hi!
I'm at the post office now. We are having a great tour. There are millions of letters here!

Love,

Be a Philatelist

Have the children ask their families to save the cancelled stamps from their mail. Make a bulletin board or poster of the different kinds of stamps. See which stamp is the biggest, most colorful, etc.

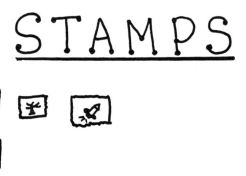

ZIP Codes

ZIP codes tell the postal workers to which areas of the country mail goes. Make a copy of the "Pat the Postman" worksheet for each child. Say, "Pat the Postman can't deliver these letters because he can't read the ZIP codes. Go over the ZIP code numerals. Say each number to yourself as you write it. Do you know your ZIP code? Write it in the boxes at the bottom of the worksheet."

Observing Spring

Many classroom spring-observation products are available. The following items can be found in the science section of various teachers' supply catalogs:

- *Root Garden* A wooden box with a clear plastic window allows children to view the development of a plant's root system.
- *Ant Farm* This is an escape-proof plastic home for ants. Children can observe the ants march, forge, explore, and build. The product includes a coupon for the ants.
- *Butterfly Garden* Through a large plastic window, the children can observe the life cycle of the butterfly. It includes a coupon to send for larvae.
- *Tadpole to Frog* This kit gives the children an exciting opportunity to watch a tadpole develop into a frog. It includes a coupon to send for a live tadpole.

There are some state shipping restrictions, so check your catalogs for details.

Miss Caterpillar and Her Cocoon

Make a copy of the "Miss Caterpillar and Her Cocoon" worksheet for each child. Say, "In the spring, caterpillars hatch from tiny eggs and begin to eat, and eat, and eat! When the caterpillar has grown as much as it can, it makes itself a cocoon. Color Miss Caterpillar and her cocoon on the worksheet. Cut them out. Fold the cocoon on the dotted line and staple the side together. After Miss Caterpillar has finished feasting, fold her in half and put her in the cocoon. Do you know what will happen to Miss Caterpillar in her cocoon?"

Read *The Very Hungry Caterpillar*. (See "April Storytime.")

Arbor Day

The last Friday in April is Arbor Day. Discuss with the children all the foods and products we get from trees, including fruits, wood, syrup, nuts, chewing gum, paper, and rubber. Trees also provide a home for many animals and birds. They are beautiful, too. If you can find a good-sized tree stump around the school, point out the tree rings to the children. Explain that each ring represents a year in a tree's life. Together, count the rings to see how old the tree was.

Make a copy of the "Tree Rings" worksheet for each child. Say, "Count the tree rings on these trees. Go over the rings with your brown crayon or marker. Now color the wood yellow."

Nature at Work

Trees and plants soak up water and minerals from the earth to feed their branches and leaves. For an experiment to demonstrate this concept, cut a celery stalk about an inch from its base, and set the stalk in a glass of water with a few drops of red food coloring. By the next morning, let the children observe what has happened (the celery fibers will have soaked up the red water).

MUSIC AND MOVEMENT

A Richard Scarry Record

Richard Scarry's *What Do People Do All Day?* (Caedmon, New York) is a delightful record that explains how Betsy Bear's letter gets to Grandma's house, and offers other charming behind-the-scenes explanations. Richard Scarry's workers tell us with simplicity what they do and what happens when they do it.

Another Richard Scarry record is *Great Big Schoolhouse* (Caedmon, New York). It is a fascinating introduction to the joys of learning, and a lovely way to find out about school.

This Old Man

1. This old man, he played one.
    He played knick-knack on my thumb.
    With a knick-knack, paddy-wack, give your dog a bone.
    This old man came rolling home.
    (*roll arms around and around each other*)

2. This old man, he played two.
    He played knick-knack on my shoe.
    With a knick-knack, paddy-wack, give your dog a bone.
    This old man came rolling home.
    (*roll arms around and around each other*)

3. This old man, he played three.
    He played knick-knack on my knee.
    With a knick-knack, paddy-wack, give your dog a bone.
    This old man came rolling home.
    (*roll arms around and around each other*)

4. This old man, he played four.
    He played knick-knack on my door.
    With a knick-knack, paddy-wack, give your dog a bone.
    This old man came rolling home.
    (*roll arms around and around each other*)

5. This old man, he played five.
    He played knick-knack on my hive.
    With a knick-knack, paddy-wack, give your dog a bone.
    This old man came rolling home.
    (*roll arms around and around each other*)

6. This old man, he played six.
    He played knick-knack on my sticks.

With a knick-knack, paddy-wack, give your dog a bone.
This old man came rolling home.
(*roll arms around and around each other*)

7. This old man, he played seven.
    He played knick-knack up in heaven.
    With a knick-knack, paddy-wack, give your dog a bone.
    This old man came rolling home.
    (*roll arms around and around each other*)

8. This old man, he played eight.
    He played knick-knack on my gate.
    With a knick-knack, paddy-wack, give your dog a bone.
    This old man came rolling home.
    (*roll arms around and around each other*)

9. This old man, he played nine.
    He played knick-knack on my spine.
    With a knick-knack, paddy-wack, give your dog a bone.
    This old man came rolling home.
    (*roll arms around and around each other*)

10. This old man, he played ten.
    He played knick-knack all over again.
    With a knick-knack, paddy-wack, give your dog a bone.
    This old man came rolling home.
    (*roll arms around and around each other*)

Hoppity, Hop

This game can be played with five children at a time. Cut out the carrot cards on the worksheet. Hold them upside-down in your hand. Have each child close his or her eyes and pick a card. One at a time, the children should count their cards and bunny-hop (two feet together) that many hops. Repeat once more. The child who has hopped the most number of times wins. Choose five more children and repeat.

SONGS, POEMS, AND FINGERPLAYS

Open, Shut Them

Open, shut them. Open, shut them. (*open and close fingers*)
Give them a little clap. (*clap*)
Open, shut them. Open, shut them. (*open and close fingers*)
Lay them in your lap. (*put hands on lap*)
Walk them, walk them, walk them (*move fingers upward*)
Right up to your chin. (*put fingers on chin*)
Open up your little mouth (*open mouth*)
But do not let them in! (*shake finger in "no" fashion*)

I'm a Little Teapot

> I'm a little teapot, short and stout.
> Here is my handle. Here is my spout. (*put one hand on waist;*
>   *hold the other hand out to make spout*)
> When I get all steamed up, hear me shout.
> Tip me over and pour me out. (*bend sideways at waist*)
> I'm a very special pot, it is true.
> Here, let me show you what I can do. (*stand in teapot position*)
> I can change my handle and my spout. (*switch hands*)
> Tip me over and pour me out. (*bend sideways at waist*)

_____ FROM BUTTON'S COUNTRY KITCHEN _____

Refrigerator Pudding

1 cup powdered sugar
4 tablespoons butter or margarine
4 eggs, separated

12 ladyfinger cookies or pieces of
   sponge cake
1 teaspoon vanilla

Beat together the butter and sugar. Beat the egg yolks and stir them into the butter/sugar mixture. Whip the egg whites stiff and blend in. Add the vanilla. Line a mold with the ladyfingers or strips of sponge cake. Pour the egg mixture into the mold. Cover and chill for 12 hours or longer.

Carrot Salad

Wash several fresh carrots. Grate them into a bowl. Add raisins. Mix in some honey or mayonnaise.

Potato Latkes

4–5 medium potatoes
1 medium onion, chopped
3 tablespoons flour
1 teaspoon salt

¼ teaspoon pepper
2 eggs
oil

Peel and grate the potatoes. Put the grated potatoes in a colander and press the potatoes with a wooden spoon to squeeze out as much liquid as possible. Put the potatoes into a large bowl. Add the onion, flour, salt, and pepper. Beat the eggs in a cup and add the eggs to the potato mixture. Mix well. Heat the oil in a frying pan. Form the mixture into patties and fry for 5 minutes on each side. Drain on paper towels. Serve with apple sauce.

Baked Rice Pudding

½ cup uncooked rice   ½ cup raisins
½ cup sugar   ⅛ teaspoon nutmeg
½ teaspoon salt

Preheat the oven to 275°F. Grease a 2–quart baking dish with butter or margarine. Combine the rice, milk, sugar, and salt. Mix and pour into the baking dish. Bake uncovered for 1 hour, stirring several times. Add raisins and continue to bake for another 2½ hours or until a brown film covers the top of the pudding. Sprinkle with nutmeg before serving.

VIDEOS FOR APRIL

The Velveteen Rabbit (Looking Glass Video Library, Random House)

Meryl Streep narrates this touching video about a toy rabbit that becomes real through the love of a young boy. Approximate running time: 30 minutes.

The Tale of Peter Rabbit (Golden Book Video, Western Publishing Co., 1985)

This is a cute springtime video with a lesson. Mother Rabbit warns her little ones "Don't go into Mr. McGregor's garden!" Peter disobeys and learns how wise Mother is when he survives a classic encounter with the cranky Mr. McGregor. Approximate running time: 30 minutes.

Also included on this tape are *Polly's Pet* and *The Little Red Hen*.

WORKSHEETS FOR APRIL

The following worksheets are referred to in this month's readiness activities.

Passover Foods

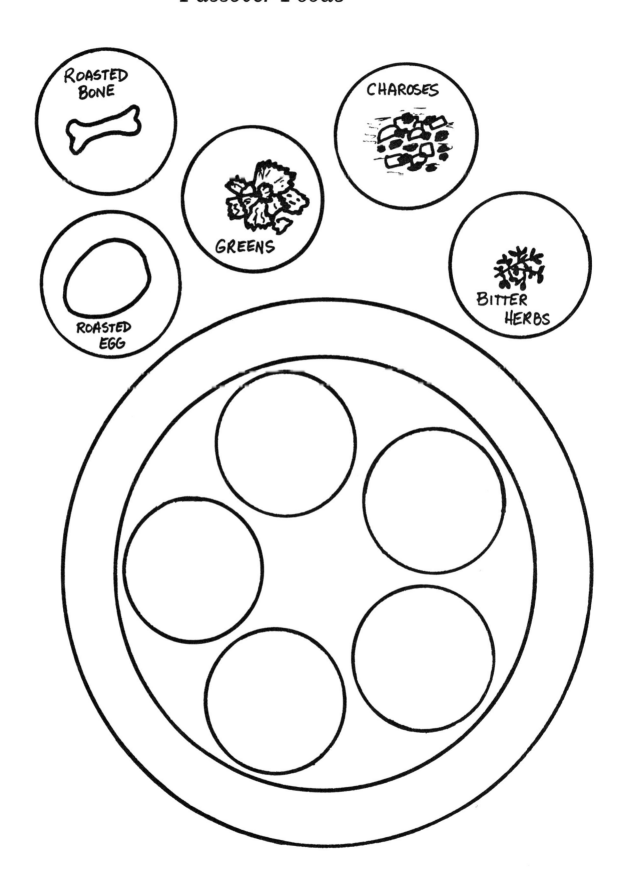

Count and Color

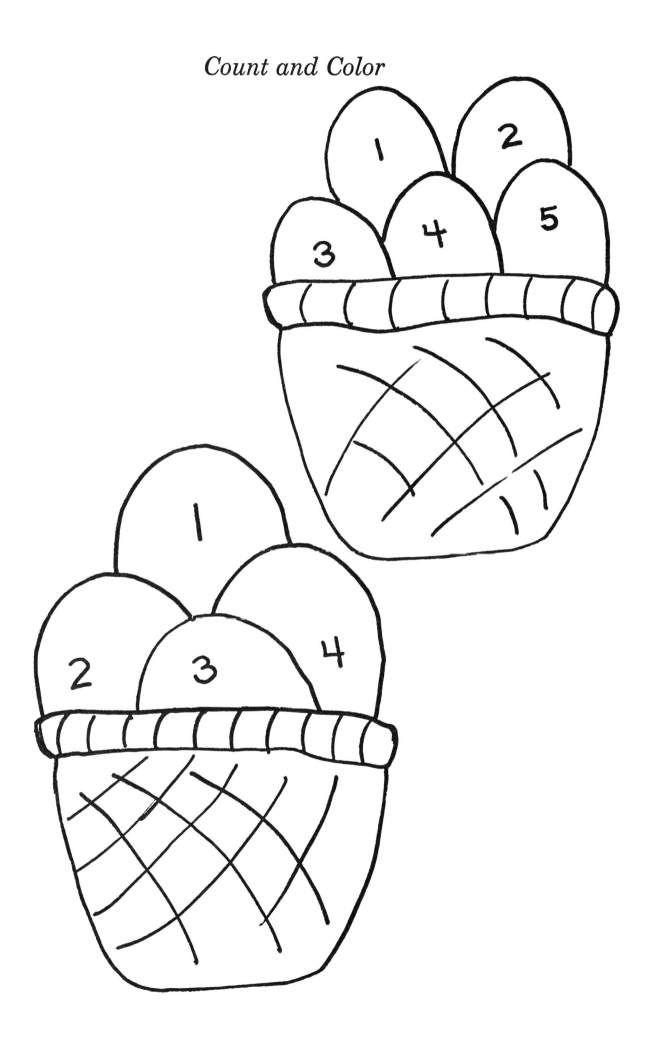

Cute-as-a-Button Bunny

Raindrops

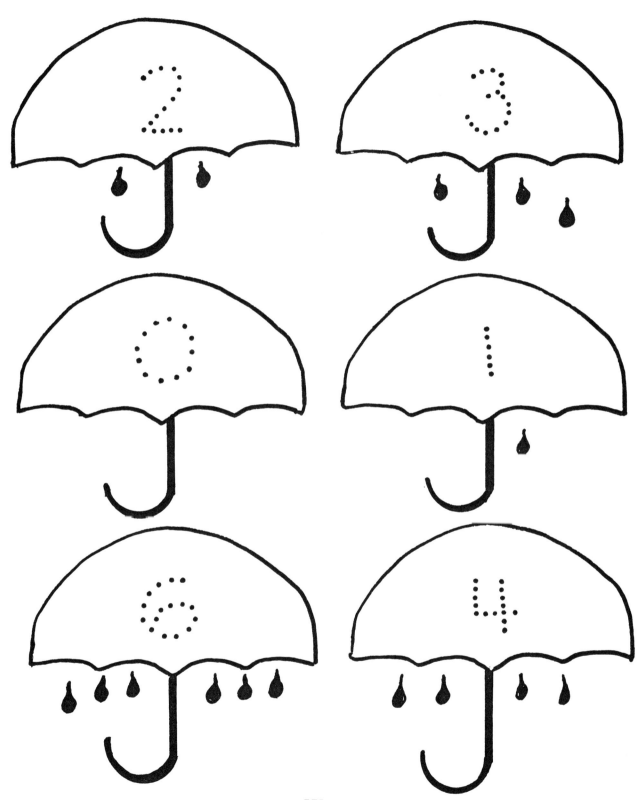

Musical Preschool
Fiddlers Lane
Harmony, PA
16037

We ♥ U Preschool
Aorta Drive
Hart, MI
49420

Grass Roots
Preschool
Lawn Street
Greenville, KY
42345

Aqua Preschool
10 Water St.
Ocean PK, WA
98640

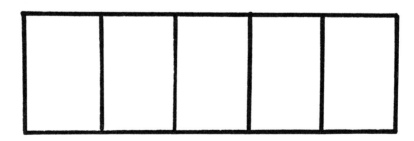

Miss Caterpillar and Her Cocoon

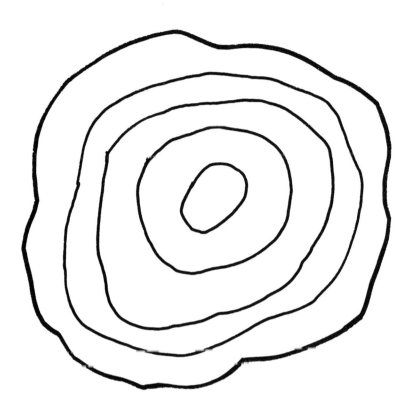

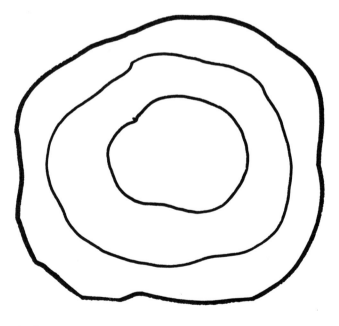

254

May/June—
An Upbeat Ending

Strike up the band—and say hurray for pre-school! As our school year comes to a close, you can look back with pride at the wonderful strides the children have made in their social and motor skills—and, most importantly, in their development of positive and secure self-esteem.

Beginnings

MAY/JUNE

Dear Parents:

As we begin to conclude our preschool year, we want to extend our thanks to you for sharing your little one with us.

This month we will be engaged in a potpourri of activities—from ladybugs and butterflies to flowers and friends.

It's been a busy and joyful school year. The children have grown and blossomed beautifully.

Sincerely,

The following books will help to increase your children's awareness and appreciation for the living things around them.

Rock-a-Bye Crocodile by JOSE ARVEGO AND ARIANE DEWEY (Greenwillow Books)

A captivating retelling of a classic Philippine fable, the story finds two boars of opposing personalities dealing with life in the jungle. Kindness and cheerfulness win over meanness and selfishness.

Frederick by LEO LIONNI (Pantheon Books)

Frederick is a delightfully different kind of book that tells of an intellectual mouse's approach to preparing for winter. Instead of gathering and storing food supplies for the cold, dark weather ahead, Frederick gathers sun rays, colors, and words. This gentle story is illustrated with gaiety and charm.

After reading this story, have the children do the "M Is for Mouse" activity.

The Pop-Up Mice of Mr. Brice by THEO. LE SIEG (Random House)

Mr. Brice and his houseful of mice pop out to teach color, number, and letter concepts. With each tab you pull, you will see these playful mice dancing, playing the guitar, and hiding in Mr. Brice's special house.

Blueberries for Sal by ROBERT McCLOSKEY (Viking Press)

This is a delightful story about picking blueberries. Kuplink, kuplank, kuplunk go the berries! A boy and his mother, and a cub and its mother enjoy a day on Blueberry Hill—eating and listening.

Have the children make some "blueberries" from blue clay or salt dough with blue food coloring added. (Remind the children that these berries are *not* for eating.) To make the salt dough, mix together 4 cups of flour, 1 cup salt, and 1½ cups water. Add some blue food coloring. Knead and form into blueberries. Bake at 300°F for 1 hour to harden, or let them air dry for one day. The children can put these into small baskets.

Conrad's Castle by BEN SHECTER (Harper & Row)

Conrad has built a sandcastle in the air. When his friend tells him "that's impossible," Conrad develops a twinge of doubt and his sandcastle crumbles. He declares "I can!" and rebuilds his sandcastle in the air.

Have the children do the "Sandcastle" worksheet after reading this story together.

Big, Small, Short, Tall by LOREEN LEEDY (Holiday House)

Up, down, near, and far—this book of opposites is a graphic teaching tool. Interesting illustrations do a great job to arouse the children's curiosity about opposites.

Oh, My, a Fly! by JAN PIENKOWSKI (Price/Stern/Sloan)

This funny book is about the "Old Lady Who Swallowed a Fly." It is a silly book that will make everyone laugh.

In the Forest by Q. L. PEARCE AND W. J. PEARCE (Silver Press)

This book introduces a variety of forest animals. Given a few simple facts and a footprint, the children are on their way to finding an animal in its natural habitat.

More Bugs in Boxes by DAVID A. CARTER (Simon & Schuster)

This is a pop-up book with pizzazz! Unusual colorful bugs pop out from a variety of boxes. The text is simple. This is a good book to complement any color recognition project.

The Wheels on the Bus by MARYANN KOVALSKI (Little, Brown & Co.)

This humorous story is an adaptation of the traditional song, "The Wheels on the Bus." (See May/June's "Songs, Poems, and Fingerplays.") The fresh, exuberant illustrations capture the bustle and funny antics that take place aboard the bus as it rides around town.

Swimmy by LEO LIONNI (Pinwheel Books/Knopf/Pantheon)

Outstanding paint prints set an unusual underwater mood. The story is about the wonder and beauty of life underwater and the courage to explore.
Other captivating books about fish include: *Fish Is Fish* by Leo Lionni (Random House), *One Fish, Two Fish, Red Fish, Blue Fish* by Dr. Seuss (Beginner Books), and *If You Were a Fish* by S. J. Calder (Silver Press).

The Reason for a Flower by RUTH HELLER (Grosset & Dunlap)

This beautifully decorated nonfiction book is ideal for showing children the variety of flowers that exist. Seeds, roots, and flower byproducts are explored.
This book is a nice introduction to this month's flower projects.

———— READINESS ACTIVITIES FOR MAY/JUNE ————

Pretty Priscilla the Butterfly

Make a copy of the "Pretty Priscilla the Butterfly" worksheet for each child. Say, "Miss Caterpillar turned into a liquid in her cocoon. Now something is coming out of the cocoon. It is a butterfly! With your markers or crayons, color Priscilla's face yellow so that you can see her features. Color the rest of Priscilla with your bright, spring colors. Then cut her out. Glue a craft stick halfway up her back. Let it dry. Hold the end of the stick and move Priscilla back and forth to make her wings fly.

F Is for Fish

Fish come in hundreds of beautiful colors and shades. (See *Swimmy* in "May/June Storytime.") Make a copy of the "F Is for Fish" worksheet for each child. Say, "Color these fish with your crayons. Use bright colors. Then make a wash of one-half teaspoon of blue tempera paint in a cup of water. Paint your whole paper, going right over your fish."

Geraniums

Geraniums are a popular summer bedding plant. Many little flowers cluster together to form one big spectacular geranium flower. Examine a real flower or look closely at a picture of a geranium with your children so that they can see all the tiny buds and flowers.

Make a copy of the "Geranium" worksheet for each child. Say, "This geranium is called an ivy-leaf geranium because the shape of its leaf resembles the three-part ivy leaf. Color the geranium leaf and stem with your green crayon or marker. Put a small amount of red tempera paint in a cup or plastic lid. Dip a cotton-tip swab in the paint and paint each flower one at a time. Go over the word GERANIUM with your marker."

A Preschool-Is-Fun Flower

Make a copy of the "Preschool-Is-Fun Flower" worksheet for each child. Say, "Color the stem and leaves of the flower green. Color the flower's middle yellow. Color the petals each a different color. Then cut out the pieces and glue them onto a piece of construction paper."

Sponge-Painted Lilacs

Early English settlers brought lilac bushes to plant in America. Lilacs are one of the most common garden shrubs. Lilac bushes grow to heights of 6–15 feet. Each flower in the lilac cluster has four lobes.

Make a copy of the "Sponge-Painted Lilac" worksheet for each child. Say, "With your crayons or markers, color the lilac branches brown and the leaves green. Trace over the word LILAC. In a small cup or bowl, put a small amount of purple paint. Dip a small piece of sponge into the paint and dab it up and down around the edge of the triangle shapes at the end of each branch. Now fill in the middle."

Pretty Petals

Make a copy of the "Pretty Petals" worksheet for each child. Say, "How many petals are on each of these daisies? Count the petals and go over the number in the middle of each flower. Color the petals your favorite spring colors."

Ladybug, Ladybug

In 1989, the ladybug became New York's official State Insect. Ladybugs are often bought by farmers because they eat insects that destroy fruit trees and other plants. Most ladybugs are reddish orange with black or yellow spots.

Make a copy of the "Ladybug, Ladybug" worksheet for each child. Say, "Color the ladybug and cut it out. Tape a piece of string to its head. Hold the end of the string and run on the playground to make your ladybug fly."

How Old Are You, Ladybug?

Make a copy of the "How Old Are You, Ladybug?" worksheet for each child. Say, "Some people say you can tell how old a ladybug is by counting its spots. Count these ladybugs' spots and go over the number. Color all your ladybugs red. You can cut out the ladybugs and the numbers, and glue the number on the underside of the ladybug. Which ladybug is the same age as you?"

Make a fishing game with the ladybugs. Tape a paper clip to each ladybug's back. Make a fishing pole out of a stick, string, and magnet. Then "fish" for the ladybugs.

Community Helper—Utility Employee

Overhead electric wires are a very familiar sight to children. They need to know that they must *never* go near a broken wire dangling overhead. Explain that storms and tree limbs often break electric wires. Only workers from the utility company are allowed to go near these wires to repair them. They begin repair by first turning off the electricity.

If one of your children's parents works for the local utility company, ask him or her to visit the classroom and bring the tools, hat, gloves, etc., that a worker might use to repair the wires.

My Preschool Friends

Distribute crayons or markers and drawing paper. Have the children draw a face and body of three special preschool friends. Emphasize that we are all friends, but today we're going to draw pictures of only three of them. You can have the child tell you each friend's name so that you can write it below each drawing.

A Sandcastle

Make a copy of the "Sandcastle" worksheet for each child. Say, "Go around the outline of your sandcastle with your orange crayon. Add flags and the sun, and color them. Mix a spoonful of sand with two spoonsful of glue and enough water to make it loose enough to be painted onto the castle. Paint the sand mixture on the castle and let it dry.

M Is for Mouse

After reading *Frederick* (see "May/June Storytime"), have the children make their own mouse.

Make a copy of the "M Is for Mouse" worksheet for each child. Say, "Color the eye and nose with your markers or crayons. Color the rest of the mouse gray or lightly with your black crayon. Cut out the mouse and fold it on the dotted line. To make its tail, lay a 6–inch piece of black yarn in the fold, with 5 inches sticking out. Glue the mouse closed. Now make a swiss cheese wedge for your mouse. Cut a piece of yellow paper to look like a wedge of cheese. Use a hole punch to make a lot of holes so that it looks like swiss cheese."

Mother's Day Plaque

Make a copy of the "Mother's Day Plaque" worksheet for each child. Have the children carefully color the border of this heart. The children should press their hand into a shallow plate of tempera paint or onto a nontoxic stamp pad, and "print" their handprint over the poem. Make a hanger with a piece of yarn or ribbon. Then glue the heart onto a piece of oaktag and cut it out.

Father's Day Card

Make a copy of the "Father's Day Card" worksheet for each child. Say, "Color the balloons each a different color. Cut out the card on the solid lines. Carefully cut out the circle. Fold on the dotted line. Write I LOVE YOU on the front of the card. Have the children decorate their cards with flowers, stripes, dots, or anything else their father would like."

Buzzy Bee

Make a copy of the "Buzzy Bee" worksheet for each child. Say, "Let's make this finger puppet. Color Buzzy with yellow and black stripes on its body. Color the wings. Then cut out Buzzy. Attach a pipe cleaner as shown. Bend Buzzy's head and wings up slightly. Have the children put their index finger in the loop and let Buzzy buzz around town!"

Fireflies

Make a copy of the "Fireflies" worksheet for each child. Say, "Fireflies are certain kinds of beetles that light up! Fireflies are also called lightning bugs and glowworms. Look at the worksheet. These three children wanted a closer look at fireflies. They each caught some and put them in jars that had holes in the lids. Count the fireflies in each jar and go over the numeral. Which jar has the most fireflies? Which has the least? The children are kind to the fireflies. After they looked closely at these interesting beetles, they let them go. Count how many bugs there are all together."

Pasta Chain

Ditali pasta is good for this project because the holes are wide enough for the pasta to be easily strung. Use a piece of yarn long enough to allow for knotting at the end and for slipping over the head of the child. Tie one piece of pasta on the end of the yarn. Knot the other end to make it easier to thread on the pasta pieces.

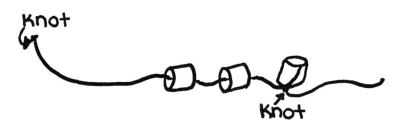

You and Me, a Math Game

You can play this game with the children individually, or with a few children at a time. Give each child five beans and two circle sets. Label one with the child's name and one with your name.

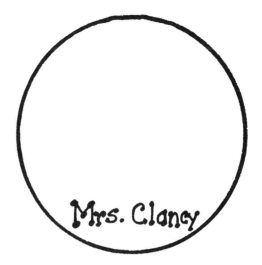

Give verbal directions:

How many beans do you have in your circle? (5)
How many beans do I have in my circle? (0)
Please give me two beans.

How many beans do you have now? (3)
How many beans do I have? (2)
Now give me one more.
How many do I have now? (3)
How many do you have? (2)
Continue. . . .

MUSIC AND MOVEMENT

Old MacDonald Had a Farm

Find pictures of various animals (cow, sheep, pig, duck, horse, dog, cat, rooster, hen, etc.), cut them out, and glue each one on a craft stick. Give one to each child. Have the children sit in a circle and sing "Old MacDonald Had a Farm." When their animal is mentioned (you might want to hold up a matching animal picture so they know what animal to sing), they get up and walk around the circle, then return to their spots.

Jack in the Box

My name is Jack (*squat with hands on head*)
I live in a box.
If you press my nose
I'll pop out. (*teacher goes around and touches each child's nose; child pops up with arms extended upward and says "pop"*)

The Snail

Children join hands and sing "The Snail." A leader marches around and around in a ring and the others follow. Continue until the leader reaches the center. After the snail is wound up, the children raise their arms in the air and shout "Hurray!" Then they let go of each other's hands.

> Hand in hand you can see us well,
> Creep like a snail into its shell.
> Closer, closer,
> Closer still.
> Very snug indeed you dwell.
> Snail within your tiny shell.
> Hurray!

Bluebird, Bluebird

Choose one child to be the first Bluebird. The rest of the children should stand in a circle and hold hands with their arms up. The Bluebird flys in and out as the children sing:

> Bluebird, bluebird, in and out my window;
> Bluebird, bluebird, in and out my window;
> Bluebird, bluebird, in and out my window;
> Oh, (Johnny), I am tired.

The Bluebird stops and stands behind a child (Johnny) and taps him on the shoulders. The children continue singing:

Take a little girl (boy) and tap her (him) on the shoulder;
Take a little girl (boy) and tap her (him) on the shoulder;
Take a little girl (boy) and tap her (him) on the shoulder;
Oh, (Johnny), I am tired.

The Bluebird and the child change places. Repeat the song until all the children have a turn as Bluebird.

——————— SONGS, POEMS, AND FINGERPLAYS ———————

The Wheels on the Bus

Be sure to read the story *The Wheels on the Bus* (see "May/June Storytime") either before or after this activity.

1. The wheels on the bus go 'round, 'round, 'round
    (*make circular motions with hands*)
    'Round, 'round, 'round, 'round, 'round, 'round,
    The wheels on the bus go 'round, 'round, 'round,
    All over town.

2. The wipers on the bus go swish, swish, swish
    (*move arms back and forth*)
    Swish, swish, swish, swish, swish, swish,
    The wipers on the bus go swish, swish, swish,
    All over town.

3. The horn on the bus goes beep, beep, beep
    (*press hand on horn*)
    Beep, beep, beep, beep, beep, beep,
    The horn on the bus goes beep, beep, beep,
    All over town.

4. The babies on the bus go waa, waa, waa
    (*open mouths wide*)
    Waa, waa, waa, waa, waa, waa,
    The babies on the bus go waa, waa, waa,
    All over town.

5. The seats on the bus go bump, bump, bump
    (*jump up and down*)
    Bump, bump, bump, bump, bump, bump,
    The seats on the bus go bump, bump, bump,
    All over town.

Little Bird

I saw a little bird
Go hop, hop, hop. (*make index and middle fingers hop*)

I told the little bird
To stop, stop, stop (*hold up hand*)
And away he flew. (*put hand behind back*)

The Little Turtle

There was a little turtle who lived in a box.	(*make box with index fingers and thumbs of both hands*)
He swam in a puddle and he climbed on the rocks.	(*make swimming motion, then climbing motion*)
He snapped at a mosquito, he snapped at a fly.	(*make grabbing motion*)
He snapped at a minnow and he snapped at me.	(*make grabbing motion*)
He caught the mosquito and he caught the fly.	(*shake head "yes"*)
He caught the minnow, but he didn't catch me!	(*shake head "no"*)

FROM BUTTON'S COUNTRY KITCHEN

Banana Slush

You will need one-half banana for each child. Peel the bananas and freeze them overnight. Cut the bananas into approximately one-inch pieces. Put them in a blender and blend until slushy. You can use a little milk to make a smoother consistency. Pour into small cups and enjoy.

VIDEOS FOR MAY/JUNE

Good Morning, Good Night: A Day on the Farm (Bo Beep Productions)

This 20–minute video uses delightful imagery, and is designed with children's developmental needs in mind. The action is set to music but is not narrated, so that you can interact with the children and the video. A guide is included to give suggestions for follow-up activities.

The Pokey Little Puppy and the Patchwork Blanket (Golden Book Video, Western Publishing, 1985)

This is a perky springtime story with a message of sharing. The Pokey Little Puppy romps through the spring meadow, leaving pieces of his blanket everywhere.

Happily, Pokey learns about sharing when his brothers and sisters help Mother make a new blanket.

This 30–minute video also includes *The Sailor Dog* and *Little Toad to the Rescue.*

A Day at Old MacDonald's Farm (Kidsongs Videos from View-Master)

These upbeat melodies and classic lyrics encourage children to sing and dance along with the cast. The songs include "Mary Had a Little Lamb" and "Take Me Out to the Ballgame." Approximate running time: 25 minutes.

WORKSHEETS FOR MAY/JUNE

The following worksheets are referred to in this month's readiness activities.

Pretty Priscilla the Butterfly

F Is for Fish

Geranium

GERANIUM

PRESCHOOL
IS
FUN !

Sponge-Painted Lilac

LILAC

Pretty Petals

273

Ladybug, Ladybug

How Old Are You, Ladybug?

Sandcastle

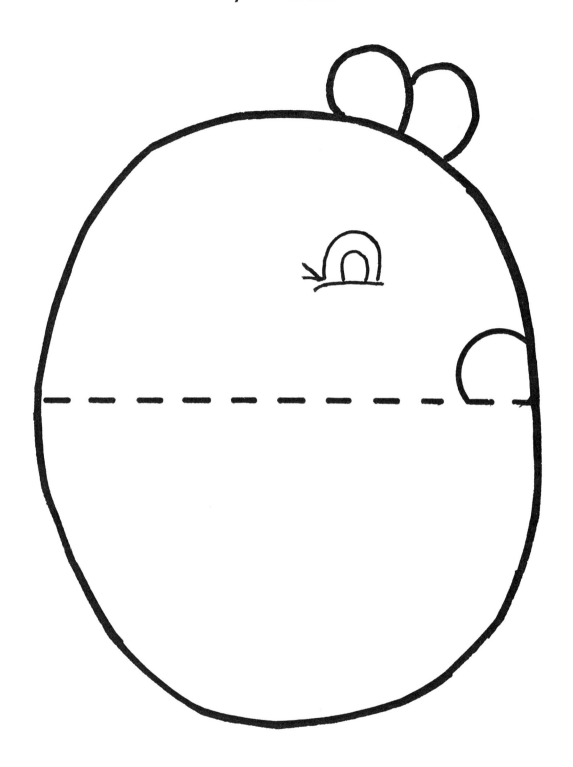

Mother's Day Plaque

Here is my preschool handprint, just for you.
Do you know what my little hands can do?
I can color and draw and hold my straw.
I can throw a ball.
But most of all
I can use them to hug my Mom
Whom I love so!

Happy Mother's Day!
Love,

_____

A WHOLE BUNCH!

Buzzy Bee

1. Insert pipe cleaner from bottom.

2. Leave enough room for an index finger.

twist

3. Twist on top. Insert index finger into the loop on the bottom.

Fireflies